KARMA HEALING

"Yael Eini explores in depth a fresh perspective on what karma is and, as importantly, ways you can release yourself from the bonds of past life experiences that have continued to find expression in the present. She describes various techniques that you can use to shed these influences that may have inhibited you in fully becoming who you are meant to become."

~ **STEVEN FARMER**, PH.D., psychotherapist, shamanic healer, and author of *Healing Ancestral Karma* and *Animal Spirit Guides*

"Yael's book resonates deeply with my evolved somatic therapeutic practice. Her straightforward teachings and the simple yet profound Karmic Constellation processes she outlines provide invaluable insights and tools for seekers and practitioners alike. These methods offer efficient mental and spiritual pathways for personal transformation and healing. *Karma Healing* is a must-read if you consider yourself an open-minded human on the path to deeper self-awareness and healing."

~ **BRIGIT VIKSNINS**, MAT, RCST, SEP, BCTMB, founder of Alchemical Alignment and coauthor of *The Map of Seven Realms*

"Satisfaction arrives when we make the move from a life dictated by karma to living our own true destiny. This beautiful book shares practical ways of working with the body to create such significant shifts."

~ **JULIA PAULETTE HOLLENBERY**, bodyworker, therapist, and author of *The Healing Power of Pleasure*

"*Karma Healing* is an inspiring tapestry of personal reflections, case studies, and profound wisdom that reveals the limitless possibilities of our journey. As we navigate life's challenges that arise at the soul level, it's important to acknowledge the deep healing that comes from our experiences. Yael Eini invites us to shift our perspectives and explore our soul's journey in a new light. Through her Karmic Constellation approach, she beautifully combines soul work with the valuable tools first introduced in family constellation therapy, offering us an innovative yet compassionate pathway to healing. I strongly recommend this book to anyone ready to deepen their soul journey and heal."

~ **EFRAT SHOKEF**, PH.D., social-organizational psychologist, shamanic energy healing practitioner, and author of *The Promise We Made: Three Universal Soul Promises We Made to Our Children*

KARMA HEALING

Unblock Your Life on the Soul Level

Yael Eini

FINDHORN PRESS

Findhorn Press
One Park Street
Rochester, Vermont 05767
www.findhornpress.com

Findhorn Press is a division of Inner Traditions International

Disclaimer
The information in this book is given in good faith and intended for
information only. Neither author nor publisher can be held liable by any
person for any loss or damage whatsoever which may arise from the use of
this book or any of the information therein.

Cataloging-in-Publication data for this title is available from the Library of Congress

ISBN 979-8-88850-259-4 (print)
ISBN 979-8-88850-260-0 (ebook)

Printed and bound in the United States by Lake Book Manufacturing, LLC

10 9 8 7 6 5 4 3 2 1

Cover and inside illustration by VectorART, Adobe Stock
Edited by Nicky Leach
Text design and layout by Anna-Kristina Larsson
This book was typeset in Garamond, Spartan MB, Tokyo Dreams, and
Roxborough CF

To send correspondence to the author of this book, mail a first-class letter
to the author c/o Inner Traditions • Bear & Company, One Park Street,
Rochester, VT 05767, USA and we will forward the communication,
or contact the author directly at **www.yaeleini.com**.

In January 2023, my father, Michael Greenberg,
passed away after a long battle with cancer.

My talent for writing and deep love of the written word was
inherited from him. I also owe my vocation as an emotional
therapist to him. My soul chose my father so that he could
help me develop certain qualities that I could later share
with the world in order to help others.

This book is dedicated to him.

CONTENTS

What if, in one lifetime, you could reincarnate more than once without dying? Simply connect to the source of creation and, from there, set out on a journey and return. More than once in one lifetime. This is our invitation for you to embark on a journey.

This symbol represents the great sun, the evolution of the soul, and the infinite cycle of reincarnation. Going back and forth to come from the great sun, from the source and creation, to go out into the world and return again.

— The Group

THE PATH

The eternal Tao
cannot be captured by words
Trying to give it a name
will fail to reveal its true core

Nameless
is the source
of Heaven and Earth
Without title
is the mother
of ten thousand things

Blinded by desires
you will only see the external things
Without desires
you will also be able to see the unseen

There are many things in the world
With different names for them all
But there is only one big mystery
both behind and beyond

The great mystery and the world of
    things
differ by name
yet their origin is the same
Springing from one single source

Live without fear
Feel the world
Experience the obstacles
Know this world

Beyond
The gate
Of
Phenomena
Flows
The river
Of
Tao[1]

---

1 Lao Tsu, *The Book of Tao: Tao Te Ching*. Translation by Nissim Amon. Contento de Semrik, 2005, p. 1.

PREFACE

If someone had told me in the year 2000 that I'd be a healer and medium and deal with topics like karma and past lives, I would probably have burst out laughing and it would have taken me hours to calm down. When I look back, I am struck by the way I changed the course of my life—by the fact that I did not let past traumas, the patterns I was born into, and the social narratives that shaped me dictate the course of my life.

Dropping karma means exactly what it implies—leaving patterns, traumas, and constructed social narratives to actively create your own life. Consistently noticing who and what is controlling you, whether or not you are content where you are, and asking to be released from that which prevents you from realizing your essence so that you may authentically express yourself in the way that best serves you.

Dropping karma means being the creator of your own existence rather than letting the recent, distant, intergenerational, or soul-based past run your life. Sometimes it happens magically; most of the time it takes work. Karma does not change on its own. It changes when we work to change it.

I see how I did it—how I dropped my own karma—and I did it more than once. I won't lie. It was often a struggle. I stumbled along the way. I searched for my path and frequently felt that instead of stepping forward I was moving backward, that

15

instead of comfortably driving a Tesla, I was riding a llama on a narrow rocky road on the edge of a looming cliff.

I am sometimes taken by these sentiments, even today. Dropping karma doesn't mean that I'm transformed overnight from an angry and irritable person into an inclusive, loving, and compassionate person who is not at all affected by the past (familial and karmic) and behaves like a tabula rasa (blank slate), devoid of history, living solely in the present. Changing karma is a process during which, each time, we again shed something from within ourselves. We cleanse some part of the patterns and traumas that control us. We replace some of the provisions in our backpacks, but not all of them.

Not every change we go through in our lives is a karmic change. Changing karma is about choice: deciding to act in a certain way and carrying out that decision. In my case, I think it started when I was 13 ½. One evening, while I was roughhousing with my younger brother on the carpet, laughing and fighting in turn, my father blew up at us, shouting and demanding that we stop this wild behavior immediately. I didn't listen to him. I was so preoccupied with my brother and what I wanted from him that my father's words simply went over my head. At some point, my father lost his patience completely, came up to me, pulled me away from my brother, and raised his hand over me. He didn't hit me—he was just about to hit me—and I took this opportunity to change the course of my life and realize a dream I had held back, inside myself, for several years. The dream was to leave home.

The realization of this dream was problematic. Where would a 10- or 13-year-old girl go? How would I live? How would I survive? These questions kept me from leaving home. On the kibbutz, when children reach the age of 13, they receive a kind of shared housing unit in which they are together (two in a room) after school and until the afternoon, however they are not allowed to sleep in this unit nor are they allowed to live in it.

The moment my father raised his hand to me I decided that I'd thumb my nose at everyone, disregard the kibbutz's decisions, and go to sleep in the housing unit, paying no mind to the shame my parents would confront by my "running away." I conditioned my return home (as in, I'd agree to stop living in the housing unit) upon their promise that I be sent to boarding school.

It took a few weeks, during which everyone around me was appalled by my unconventional actions and the embarrassment I was causing my parents. Just to clarify, at the time, boarding school was considered, at least according to the kibbutz worldview, a place for disturbed children or children from difficult homes, so the fact that I, a good girl, wanted to go to boarding school shook people's worlds. In addition, my refusal to speak to my parents or to come home saddled them with shame, and this in an environment where everyone aims to be like everyone else, was not an easy thing for people.

But I had decided. I decided I was changing my life. I was no longer going to be a victim of my parents and a victim of the kibbutz, and the only way out was to go to boarding school. So I got up, left the house I'd known and the kibbutz where I'd lived, and moved into a boarding school for two years. During these years I was exposed to a different population from the one I grew up with and developed into a different being.

Leaving the kibbutz and my parents' house saved my life.

At another and more advanced stage of my life, when I studied trauma therapy using the Somatic Experiencing method, I realized that my life experience as a child on the kibbutz evoked a feeling of being imprisoned. The kibbutz was a confined space I could not escape—socially, emotionally, or physically. Unlike a prison, it was not surrounded by walls, guards, or barbed wire, but it was far from a supportive environment. As a 13-½-year-old girl, boarding school was a drastic choice and totally out of the question by kibbutz norms. In order to accept such an extreme choice something extreme had to precede it, so I turned my experience with my father into something extreme.

I'm not sure what force motivated me to do it. It was the desperate act of a miserable girl who hated her life and felt trapped at home and in the kibbutz. A girl who no one understood, who no one listened to. A lonely girl in a closed society, in a home where both parents were too focused on themselves to see her and to notice her distress.

I am almost certain that had I stayed on the kibbutz I would not be alive today.

Leaving the kibbutz changed my life. Looking back, I think it was the defining event of my life; it taught me that I have the power to change and am responsible for my life. I have been on a constant journey to change my life ever since.

Our lives change in one of two ways. One is when an external force changes it for us: Our parents decide to relocate, and we move from city to city or country to country. No one asks us. We are passive in our capacity to make decisions. The same is true in the case of illness or the death of a loved one, as well as in the case of being fired. We don't choose the disease, we don't choose the person we love dying, and we don't choose to be let go from our job. We are seemingly passive; it happens to us.

The truth is, when that happens, it's part of our karma. We choose our parents knowing that they will move and it will change our lives. The illness is there, either as a choice or a potential, in order to realize karma. It manifested itself and so did the layoffs and losses.

Many times "being in karma" means being reactive to life; that is, acting in response to what life throws at us. On this path, we will also find that karma repeats itself again and again, and we hardly evolve or change.

The second way for our lives to change is by us taking responsibility for our own life and actively changing it. We choose to move, to resign, to heal ourselves from our illness; we are the ones who make changes in our lives from a place of conscious choice. In this way, life is not something that happens to us, but rather, something that we create. And, in this way, karma can be changed and the repetition stopped.

To be able to take the second path we have to take action. We have to work to make it happen, and this often requires working through unconscious patterns and clearing past traumas, whether they be childhood traumas, traumas passed down from generation to generation, or traumas from past lives. It requires consciously and subconsciously internalizing that we deserve better.

Every time I consciously and deliberately chose to take responsibility for my life, significant changes followed. The second time I changed the course of my life was during my undergraduate studies in Psychology and Management. I dreamed of becoming an organizational consultant and looked for work in the field. It took me exactly six months to realize that what I thought about organizational consulting and the dreams I had were diametrically opposed to what I experienced in reality. I no longer wanted this dream, but I had no idea what I did want.

As part of my soul searching, I made an appointment with Navit, a medium and energy healer. Only after the fact did I realize that the encounter with Navit was a formative event in my life. Her work changed my life in three ways:

First, significant patterns of behavior that had been running my life disappeared. They vanished without Navit even knowing they were bothering me. I saw dramatic changes in my behavior. It seemed like magic to me.

Second, Navit opened my mind to the world of energy healing. Until then I had not known much about it and assumed it was completely unfounded. I treated the field as a racket. But there is no wiser teacher than experience, and my experience showed me that energy healing works.

And third, a few months after I started the process with Navit I had a mystical experience of my own. It was a routine evening and, as I was getting ready to go to bed, I felt strong energies coming out of my hands and pressing me against the mattress. Since I had already experienced energies with Navit, I knew that they were energies, but I was still surprised and didn't know what to do. Not to mention, it hurt. I asked myself, what the hell am I supposed to do with this? I had no idea.

When the feeling returned the following day, I consulted Navit. She told me that I could use the energy to send distance healing and explained to me what that meant (sending energy to people who weren't physically around me). On the third day, when the experience repeated itself, I sent the energies that came out of my hands to my grandmother, who lay unconscious in the hospital. I don't know if the energies I sent her helped her or not but, on a personal level, those days changed my life. It was clear to me that the world of energy healing was where I belonged, and I began to walk this path.

Looking back, I can say that the magic of energy healing happened for me because I was primed for it. I came open and ready, so I experienced significant changes after just the first meeting. As an emotional and energetic therapist who synthesizes diverse modalities in the clinic (healing, Somatic Experiencing, Family and Karmic Constellations, and the Akashic Records), I see magic all the time. At the same time, this magic happens to those who are prepared for it. This readiness can be fully conscious, or it can exist on the soul level, which is subconscious and inaccessible to the client.

One of the greatest and most significant changes I made for myself was in the world of parenting, and my biggest fear was becoming a parent like my parents.

As a child, I suffered. The environment I grew up in was not a safe space for me. I had a father who took his anger out on us unpredictably (never knowing when or how this would occur or what would instigate it), and an inattentive mother who didn't understand me. I didn't want to turn out like my father or my mother. When I became a mother myself, fear was a compulsion, and it was my biggest motivator. I asked myself what I must do so as not to become my parents, at least in ways that deeply bothered me. Later, this became my occupation and my passion: healing parents so that their children don't experience a painful childhood like mine.

It's not always easy. Often, it's not that simple. "Dropping" or "changing" karma sounds like fun and games, but the truth is that it's not always like that. Many times the change comes from a position of great distress. It originates from no longer being able to tolerate where we are, in our life or in our environment.

I struggled not to be like my parents. I worked on it and invested in it. It was the most meaningful work I've ever done in my life, and I see it as the total expression of changing karma. While my parents, in many ways, followed in their parents' footsteps, I feel that even though I belong to my parents and their lineage, I've made changes in my life and in the lives of my children. That, for me, is the essence of changing karma.

In the Mishnah, the oldest post-biblical collection of Jewish oral laws, there is a line that describes the experience of free will and karma very nicely: "All is foreseen, and freedom of choice is granted." (Avot 3:15) My soul chose my parents. What my parents would give me was foreseen. How I choose to react to what they give me is the granted permission. This is the unexpected.

We are four siblings in my family. Each of us took our experience of our parents' parenting in a different direction. I took this life experience and transformed it into an offering of service to the world. I became an emotionally focused therapist for parents. In this way, I passed on the knowledge I had acquired—knowledge of dealing with anger and releasing it from my life—and created attentive and alternative parenting for thousands of parents.

These days I am on my path. I know that this didn't have to be my path—my life could have ended on the kibbutz as an angry and embittered person and parent. The freedom of choice was there all along. I chose differently. And, to this day, choice always exists. There are some issues that I haven't solved yet and am still searching my way through them, and others that I'm researching, examining, and wondering how I can change. We all have a path to follow and explore. "Life is what happens while you're busy making other plans," John Lennon said. Unwittingly, while I was intently researching the possibility of working with Family Constellations tools in more esoteric spaces such as Akashic Records, the Karmic Constellation method evolved. (The Akashic Records are a realm that holds all the knowledge of the soul from the moment it first incarnated on Earth to the present moment. It is not a physical space, like a library, but a realm that can be entered to learn about our soul journey.) I didn't plan on developing a treatment method. It wasn't by design. It developed on its own, from the depths of my being—the being of an investigative and experiential person. In truth, I only realized I had a method on my hands when one of the lab participants asked me when I'd be teaching how to work with the Constellation framework on soul themes.

How I Discovered Karmic Constellations

As I worked more with parents, more and more often I saw patterns of behavior that have existed in a family for generations. I didn't know then it was called "intergenerational transfer," but I noticed then that it bothered me, and I wanted to find a way to undo it. That's how I came to study Family Constellations.

I studied with the intent of learning how to reverse and cure intergenerational transmission and ended up falling in love with the method and what it evokes. I now had a tool. This tool could serve me in helping parents with parenting difficulties and frustrations, in addition to working with intergenerational transfer. I wanted to learn more about this tool and understand its full capabilities.

At the beginning of my professional career as an energy-focused therapist, I learned a treatment method called EMF Balancing Technique. Tamar Genesher, the teacher of the method in Israel, spoke about a man named Lee Carroll who channels an energetic being named Kryon. After class, I went to the bookstore and bought the book that was on the shelf, book number 10. Not long after I purchased the book, my beloved grandmother passed away. I took the book with me to the shiva. On the eve of her funeral, I opened the book and read a paragraph about how people leave this planet for all sorts of reasons. My grandmother was in her mid-sixties when she died. She died of medical malpractice. Kryon's message touched me deeply, and I began following his channeled messages.

In 2017, I founded the Systemic Lab, a space for exploring varied concepts from diverse fields using tools from Constellations. The goal of this space is to identify themes, work processes, deeper understandings of the constellations, and more.

About six months after the Systemic Lab was founded, I went back to reading and listening to Kryon's channeled communications. I needed them and the loving messages they contained. I suddenly became curious whether it would be possible to use representations for the Akashic Record. Would it be possible to work with such esoteric concepts?

I decided to investigate, and the answer was yes, I could.

I spent eight months in the lab studying the Akashic records and unwittingly created a method. Karmic Constellations is more than working with the Akashic records. It is work with the soul, soul lessons, past lives, contracts, vows, and all that exists within our soul's ecosystem.

In working with Karmic Constellations, I continue to discover more and more about myself and to heal fears upon fears from past lives. Karmic Constellations is constantly evolving and expanding. My students and I are always learning new processes and gaining fresh insights. This allows the constellation work to grow and expand. It is a dynamic and evolving field of work that contains a lot of healing, and I am thrilled to be the conduit of this field and, in so doing, have had the honor of helping people change their karma.

My wish is that as you read this book, you are able to change your karma as well.

The Group and the Channeled Messages in the Book

The purpose of this book is to expand your consciousness, to instill in you an abundance of possibilities and viewpoints, and to expand your perspective on the old notions of karma and how to drop them. Every example given in the book, every concept, such as soul lessons, soul contracts, vows, and so on, are concepts that accompany you as souls, as people walking on this earth. When you understand these concepts, you can expand your perspectives and even see beyond yourselves and let go of things that are holding you back. Nothing is set in stone in the world of souls, only in the world of men.

We are here to encourage you to let go of everything in your experience, conscious and especially unconscious, that is still attached, often riveted, to experiences from the past. We're here to help you let go of those rivets. Again, we say, not everything that used to be is as it should be; you have free will and choose which way to go.

— The Group

My editor and I are working on the book. She asks me to elaborate on the concept of changing karma. I'm having trouble finding the words. That which is clear in my mind and my being disappears when I sit down to write. I feel like I've written every-thing I had to say in the best way I know how. I feel helpless in the face of her lack of understanding.

Suddenly I feel an energy coming into me. A message wants to take form. I tell her to quickly start recording (thank you, Zoom and smartphones) and a message comes through from an energy that calls itself The Group. I don't know who The Group is and, I admit, it's not something that concerns me either. I'm more interested in their messages and the feeling I get when I channel them. Their energy pleases me, they convey ideas clearly, and they advance the development of this book during times when I find it difficult to convey the information.

From the moment they showed up to talk about changing karma, they went chapter by chapter with me and added their insights. Sometimes they explained the subject matter better than I did. Other times they added new information. Working with The Group was inspiring and taught me a lot. The chan-neled messages of The Group are written in a distinct font, in order to distinguish them from my writing.

The Group does not only share the content of its messages but also transmits a frequency. It is my hope and wish that when you read these words, you receive not only the channeled message but the vibrational frequency emitted beyond these words.

Love, Yael

Chapter 1
DROPPING KARMA

Most have heard the saying "Karma is a bitch." We've heard it in movies and TV shows, read it in books and social media posts, and our perception of the concept of karma is that it will catch and punish us. If I were to ask you now what karma is, you would likely say it's a judgment-based system in which we are either punished or rewarded based on our actions in our past lives.

In 2007, Kryon shared a channeled message that was deeply meaningful to me, and challenged the prevailing notion I too held, that karma is something inescapable, a kind of fate determined in part by actions taken in other lifetimes. Kryon's message had me breathe a sigh of relief for the first time and let go of old thoughts I had about karma.

> In 1989 I began to tell you that, in this new energy, you had the opportunity, if not the obligation, to get out of karma and walk the path of your choice. You have the ability to get out of the crack. You can take the old karma and put it aside, and replace it with something of a much higher energy.[2]

---

2 https://audio.kryon.com/en/K_Handbook01.mp3

Kryon is an energetic angelic being. He introduces himself as the group of angels watching over Earth's magnetic field. He began his channeling in 1989. He speaks of a new age that humanity has chosen to experience. He conveys his messages mainly through Lee Carroll, who is the man who channels and publishes him.

Kryon's channeled messages often deal with karma, working with Akashic records, raising the human frequency, and beyond. To me, his messages are missives of love and growth and, many times when I listen to him, I feel an inner truth in what he says. When he gave this channel about karma, my whole body cried out, "Yes, yes, we can let go of our karma!" I was on cloud nine. Later, when I rested, I asked myself: But how the hell do you do that?

What Is Karma?

The word karma is taken from Sanskrit. It means "action." Different religions and faiths view karma slightly differently.

The Hindu religion sees karma as cause and effect. Suffering in this incarnation is the result of being bad in your previous life.

Buddhism believes that karma is the reason why a soul reincarnates in this world. Life in this incarnation is the result of life in the previous life and determines our next incarnation.

~~~~~

The energy that's coming into the universe at this time, the energy that this book wants to bring forth, is an energy of coming out of these perceptions. We appreciate these perceptions very much but, at the

same time, this new energy seeks to break out of the
mindset that what was will influence what will be. This
new energy makes room for growth and encourages
personal choices, a personal point of view, and the
ability to change perspective.

— The Group

The concept of punishment and reward is the prevailing view when we deal with karma, and it has also been significantly reinforced over the years by the monotheistic religions—Judaism, Christianity, and Islam—which do not deal with reincarnation but speak of punishment and reward and going to Heaven or Hell.

The perception we have of karma is linear. It is a concept that looks at life in clear terms of past—present—future, in which what governs our present is, for the most part, our past, and it is also what influences our future. This linear concept of karma comes from a lifetime of conditioning: If your children make your life miserable, it's because in a previous life you made their lives miserable and you're being punished for it. It's a concept that sees life's pains as punishment for things we have done wrong at some point in our lives. This is a dichotomous and binary view of good and evil; it is black-and-white thinking that does not see things from a broader perspective and does not take into account the outcomes and ripple effects of our actions, not only in our lives here and now, but throughout our entire soul history. Finally, it is a concept that sees a person as a victim of their life. What happens to them is necessary punishment or retribution for their actions. This perspective negates our personal responsibility and our soul's choices.

On one occasion, when I listened to Lee Carroll channeling Kryon (in June 2022), he gave a beautiful explanation of karma.

Kryon's messages, by and large, expand my heart and speak high truths to me. I liked Lee's explanation, which I paraphrase here as follows:

"Karma is an energy created to push people in their lives in the direction of evolution. The purpose of karma is to get us to the right place at the right time for us to grow and develop. Karma is a cumulative energy, or the meaning of some kind of feeling/emotion, that accompanies us for this incarnation. It doesn't have to be related to a specific person."

In fact, karma is the engine of the soul and, therefore, also of man. It is the reason why the soul descends to materialize in the body. Karma is embodied through events we go through and in our relationships. It is influenced by how we deal with events and people in our lives.

Karma is the soul contract that drives us. It is our soul contract with other people. It is the reason we are here and especially, the lesson or lessons that we, our souls, came here to learn. Our cosmic journey is the journey of soul development, because from creation we came and to creation we will return. As souls, we have knowledge but lack the sense of the actual experience. The purpose of reincarnation is to deepen one's knowledge of experience through sensations and emotions.

The purpose of karma is soul growth. When we meet someone, the interaction we create with them is karma. It motivates us, it teaches us, it allows us to accumulate experiences, and it helps us to develop both as human beings and as souls. And yes, encountering the other can be painful, even very painful. At the same time, this pain is not a punishment; rather, it is an invitation to learn. The person may not learn, but the soul learns. Karma contains within it soul lessons, soul contracts, and the accumulated energy of all we've learned in previous lives.

When I was young, I loved singing (I still do). At some point in my childhood, my father told me I was singing off-key. All at once, in an instant, my self-confidence evaporated and, if until that moment I sang joyously for pleasure, as if no one could hear me, from that moment on I made sure to hide behind the voices of others.

After becoming a mother, there was a night my eldest son, about six months old, couldn't stop crying. I was tired, frightened, helpless, and alone, and I didn't know what to do. Suddenly, a vision appeared to me about life in a tribe, somewhere in another age of civilization, in past life. At that time, I hadn't worked with previous lives and wasn't really involved with therapy. A song arose from my stomach, made its way up to my throat, and emerged. My son calmed down and fell asleep. I, too, calmed down.

After my maternity leave, I started seeing clients. Suddenly, during therapy, in the middle of a session, I felt like singing. Shall I sing? Me? After all, I'm off-key! My father's voice was strongly embedded in me, but the need to sing in therapy was stronger. I apologized to my clients for the pitch and let the many sounds that wanted to come out of me be released. None of my clients thought I was off-key . . .

When my father told me what he told me, he couldn't see me and the pleasure I got from singing. He was self-absorbed. Nevertheless, what he did shifted things inside me and took me through a long process of learning. When my son cried that night, my soul and guidance took advantage of the openness (and despair) I was in to remind me and open something up that existed in me from days gone by. This motivated me to take action.

Perhaps my father's statement to me was a gift. There's a chance that this was part of my soul contract with him, and there is no doubt that it led me to personal/physical growth as Yael and soul growth. Can what happened to me with my father be defined as punishment? No doubt that was the feeling. It certainly hurt me deeply, but to look at it as punishment, as if it were repaying me for something I'd done to him in a previous life, is a narrow perspective and fails to see the long-term consequences of his act or statement.

These three stories—the story with my father, the story with my son, and my story with the field of therapy—began many processes in my life and motivated me to deal with various issues, as well as accelerating my personal development. The inner tools I have at my disposal are all connected to this incarnation and beyond that, to my past lives and karma. If karma is an accumulation of energy and experiences from past and present lives, can it be changed?

Can Karma Be Changed?

It is impossible to change what was, but it is possible to change our perspective on the events, to heal the pain, and to change the energy in the present. When this happens, karma changes.

Every person can change their life. Sometimes it will involve a big effort; other times it will be very simple. Anyone who has changed their life and is reading this book knows that it is possible. To any person who is fighting to change their life and is reading the book, I want to instill in you a sense of optimism that it is possible. What used to be doesn't have to dictate what will be—this is the Age of Changing Karma.

If you've changed things in your life, you know that it's true. It doesn't matter what happened in another life, or in previous generations, or in childhood. We know, however, that the human perspective gets stuck on these things. Your life experience is seared into your body, and it tells a story that is connected to your childhood memories, your family lineage, and your past lives. So yes, healing these things changes you. When you change yourself, the course of your life will also change.

Is it possible to change karma? Yes. How does one go about changing it? One way is to change your perspective of the past, your point of view, how you see things, and allow yourself to be released from your past. The other way is to create a new reality. What do you want to achieve? Set an intention for what you want to achieve, and say a prayer (this has nothing to do with religion)—a prayer from the innermost self to let go of and release everything that prevents you from achieving what you want to achieve: the generational history from which you came, your personal history, and your soul history. These are the two ways to change karma.

— The Group

The understanding that past life regression can heal present symptoms developed throughout the 20th century, towards the end of which saw more and more psychologists and psychiatrists embracing the incredible healing abilities of this type of therapy. Among the famous works that have influenced the world in this regard, I highly recommend the writings of Dr. Michael Newton, Dr. Brian L. Weiss, and Dr. Roger Volger (the order of the authors' names indicates the order in which they entered my life and not the importance of their work). These therapists and healers realized that when they did regression work, helping their clients revisit memories of past lives, the memories that came up were often related to physiological difficulties, phobias, anxieties, and other difficulties that the clients experienced in their current incarnation. In confronting these past traumas, wounds present in their current incarnation dissipated. Anxiety and phobias vanished, personal difficulties disappeared, and even diseases were cured.

In my experience, working with Karmic Constellations goes beyond healing the past in service of healing the present; healing the soul can actually change the future. If karma can be "dropped," as Kryon suggests, then it must first be made present in a particular way. I believe that in order to set something aside, we must have an idea of what that something is. To this end, it is necessary to bring up—that is, to represent in the therapeutic space—not only the previous incarnation but also the soul, soul lessons, contracts, vows, and all forces that drive our karma and, therefore, our current incarnation.

Hence, working with Karmic Constellations requires, among other things, working with past lives.

The Soul Realm and Past Incarnations

Reincarnation is a perception. You're so used to incarnating, you don't know how many times you've done it. Your perception is that incarnating is punishment, that "this incarnation must be completed." And yet you maintain a true zest for life, so much so that when death is at your doorstep you say, "Just a second, another moment, another minute, let me live." But you don't really live. The soul seems to anesthetize itself when it enters the body; you forget all the knowledge you came with, all the wisdom you have accumulated. We implore you—wake up. You are in the age of choice. Wake up from your coma. You don't have to be in theta, alpha, or beta waves to open up to who you are and to open the gate to all your incarnations. This knowledge is within you and available to you.

— The Group

When we talk about karma, we are necessarily talking about our past lives as well. These two concepts, "karma" and "past lives," are intertwined, in our perception and in their essence. However, when we talk about these two subjects, there are two important things to clarify.

The first clarification is about our perception of the sequence of incarnations. We are accustomed to talking about reincarnations as a linear continuum in which there is one incarnation that precedes another, and so on. But the soul world, unlike the physical world, is not a linear space. While we experience ourselves as being present here, in this moment, there is a greater "soul field" than we can comprehend, in which all the lives we have ever experienced coexist. Since the world of souls does not have the time sequence known to us as "past," "present," and "future," there is also no such concept as a "past incarnation" because this phrase deals with a linear sequence that describes something that comes before or after something else.

A second and no less important clarification concerns the fact that when I say "previous incarnation" I do not necessarily mean the incarnation that existed just before my current incarnation. Since there is no linear continuum in the world of souls, the order is insignificant. Therefore, when I talk about a previous incarnation that is related to my present, to the difficulty I am experiencing now, it can be an incarnation from 5,000 years ago after which my soul may have reincarnated several times. Any previous incarnation that is relevant to the difficulty that concerns me now can be worked with regardless of how many other lifetimes followed.

The Relevant Incarnation

I'm not looking for the previous incarnation. I'm looking for the relevant incarnation. The one that started it all or was most significant to what's happening now—to the reason why the client came to therapy in the first place. The metaphor I relate to the most is a rolling snowball. The more it rolls, the more snow it accumulates. It's not easy to stop a snowball. Usually, it crashes into something and that's how it falls apart. In order to stop this snowball, without (which is to say, "us") falling apart, you have to find out what created it before it even started rolling or find the thing that caused it to roll.

Your pain, especially significant pain, your wounds, specifically impactful or repetitive ones, birthmarks, and more, are all indications of body memory. One of the reasons you are said to be multidimensional is that at any given moment you are also your past incarnations. The very fact that you hold in your cellular memory your previous incarnations brings those incarnations to life.

They are present in your being, in your conduct. When
you look at your parents, you also see who they were in
a previous life for you. Sometimes you don't see it, but
you feel it. There's something there in the system that
isn't clear to you, but it controls you. Your mother may
be the most loving mother in the world, but it doesn't
work for you, because it's not from here, dear one, it's
not from here. And the body knows and tells you, "I'm not
comfortable, I'm not happy with my connection to this
mother. I know in my mind that she loves me, but it doesn't
work for me," because it's not from here, beloved one. It's
not from here. Yes, it is also related to intergenerational
transmission; we will not disregard its effects. And yet,
you are two souls who have chosen to descend together,
and you both have the memory of living together, with
one another.

— The Group

What The Group illustrates for us is that difficulties with our
mother, for example, may be related to past lives, to previous
experiences we had with each other as souls, and not necessarily
to the current life. The lack of connection to our mother, which
developed in our previous life, is in our cellular memory and
controls us.

When we remember, when we realize that our difficulty
lies in the soul's past and not in the present, change begins to
seep within us. Sometimes just remembering is enough, and
sometimes you have to do more in-depth work. With that, the
simple act of remembering already initiates a process of change
in our lives.

Reincarnation as a Time Capsule

Karma is energy that is carried from incarnation to incarnation. If I want to change my karma, I need to change the energy that my soul carries. Therefore, in almost every Karmic Constellations session, I bring a representation of the incarnation in which the energy that influences the current incarnation was created. What does representation or representative mean in this context? It is an object or person that represents that incarnation.

Why do we need representatives for this? I always look at the representative of the relevant incarnation as a time capsule that contains within it the energy and story that directly influenced that incarnation. If we look at the definition of a "time capsule" in Wikipedia, we find that a time capsule is a means of burying items from a given time with the stated intention that it will be opened at a later date, thereby transmitting to future humans an authentic memory of that period.

When I talk about the "relevent incarnation," I am talking about the incarnation in which that time capsule was created and in which there are key details from a specific time that are given to me to enable me to make corrections or effect a change. The details can be relationships that are relevant to the present, traumas that happened, natural disasters, and more. Including a representation of the relevant incarnation usually makes way for more information to come through and helps us understand what exactly happened in this incarnation that continues to affect the present.

Fact or Fiction?

Roger G. Volger, a Jungian psychologist and reincarnation worker, wrote in his book *Other Life, Other Self* that the subconscious mind will always provide us with stories from past lives, whether we believe in reincarnation or not.

So, you may ask, how do you know if a story from a previous life happened?

I admit that the veracity of the story does not concern me. In hypnosis therapy, the therapist will often ask for a geographic location and time period or year. The truth is that such knowledge helps authenticate the stories and calms any cognitive concerns. Sometimes our minds, or egos, need something to hold onto in order for us to believe. Faith can make a difference.

I work differently. The work I do relies largely on the perception that experiential shifts in the body create external change and that all changes happen within the framework of relationships. Therefore, I am not looking for dry facts. Nor do I care if the previous incarnation was in 1780 BC or AD 1780, or if it happened in Africa or Rome. What interests me, and what I believe creates change in a person in their life, is the lived experience. When there is a change in a person's experience, I know that healing is taking place.

Through representational work, stories emerge. When a representation of a previous incarnation is presented, a story often arises from it that illuminates what happened in that incarnation, who the client was, and what their relationship with the person they wanted to work with was in order to change the relationship in the present. For example, in a person who came to work on their soul relationship with their mother, the relevant incarnation will represent the previous relationship, the one that is relevant to this life. It doesn't have to be a parent–child relationship like it is today. Or we can see in the previous life that which happened to the person that affects them today. How did these stories come about?

When a person acts as a representative, sensations, feelings, and stories arise in them—stories they'd never known before. As a client once said to me in session: "What is this story? I don't know it, and I don't know where it came from." The fact that she didn't know the story, and wasn't sure where it even came from, already indicates that she didn't invent it, at least not consciously. What does this experience mean?

In one of the sessions I facilitated, the client stood in her representative from a previous life and felt she had no air. She choked. The longer she stood in as the representative, the more intense the experience of choking.

"How old are you?" I asked her.

"I'm small," she replied.

"And where are you, and where are your parents?"

She continued to experience the feeling of suffocation. By staying with the sensation, an image arose in her that she was in some kind of crate. Her parents put her there to hide her. As we delved deeper into the experience of the feeling of suffocation, the story gradually unfolded. Her parents put her in a box to protect her from someone, but they came back too late. She choked for lack of air.

As the story came up, the client was able to breathe better. The feeling of suffocation is familiar to the client from her life. Uncovering the story from a previous life helped the client heal an inner experience she had in this life. The realization of what happened in her previous life, that it was not directed against her, and that her parents intended to protect her, as well as the time spent in the sensation of suffocation while revealing the story, all brought healing to the client's emotions and created movement, both in the session itself as we got back to working on her relationships in the present, and in her life.

I always tell my clients that we don't know how much we know. Our subconscious contains the complete knowledge of who we are. All we have to do is ask to be open to this knowledge, to meet it, get to know it, recognize it, and listen to the story it shares. It is then that we can create a change in our experience of this knowledge. This is what creates healing in our lives in the here and now.

~~~~~~~

Your reincarnation is not some place you have to embark on a journey to reach. No, dear ones, it's here inside you. Every single cell in your physiological body carries your knowledge, your records, and your past lives. You don't need to look outside yourself to arrive; you need to connect with yourself. The information is there, and we will say that this is one of the reasons it is very easy in Karmic Constellation for the information to emerge, because all Yael asks is that you connect within and let the information arise from the body. The body, even though it is perishable and disposable, like most of your consumption in this incarnation, in this world, the body retains knowledge from previous lives. How it is done is a matter for another book, an alternative experience, and irrelevant here. A whole book could be written about it, and at the same time, any regression therapist will tell you that the body retains information from past lives.

Come in, dear ones. When you engage in representation work, memories come up. You don't even know that the memories are there, and we'll say something like this: You don't have to study Karmic Constellation to go inside the body and ask the pain what incarnation it's from. What incarnation is responsible for this wound? What do I bring with me, what have I brought with me here, what am I reliving over and over and over again inside myself? We want to say that when you create space for these questions, first, the energy will dissolve, and second, in everything, in every distress, there is already a solution present. The cells also remember health, happiness, and joie de vivre. When there is great pain, illness, or heartache, you will also ask what reincarnation it is from and what reincarnation is the cure for what you are experiencing now.

You are multidimensional; your incarnations are within you. When the soul enters the body, it enters with the Akashic records and the inner knowledge of the body. Within each body is a memory of previous bodies, even though the body is perishable. You are the capsule of knowledge. You. And you have all you need to figure out how to unlock it; the key to the lock is in your hands. All you need to find is the right path for you to use the key. And we, we are waiting for you to do that because, as you release more and more knowledge from the body, as your bodies refine and the spirit refines, this universe, and this collective, the whole galaxy, refines. For you are the universe, and the universe is you, beyond the divine or parallel to the divine. All we ask, all you are asked many times, is simply to open the lock. The key, the lock, the capsule—everything is you, and we sit and wait and rejoice every time you open a lock and something gets released. We celebrate it with you.

— The Group

The simple act of standing as representatives allows us to connect to knowledge that is within us and is not available to us on a daily basis. That's what happened when Liron came to me for a Karmic Constellations session.

Liron's Story

Liron is here to work on his difficulty with self-expression. We do Karmic Constellations and, therefore, work with representations. He feels that his difficulty expressing himself impedes the quality of his life and prevents him from expressing his full self.

Liron brings representatives for the concepts of "I," "Self," and "Expression." I chose to separate the term "Self-Expression" into two. This means that there are essentially two representations of the Self. At the moment, only I am aware of this. Liron is not aware of the doubling in representations. I'm curious to see where this will lead.

Liron begins to work with the representatives he brought and, while working with them, I have a strong experience of being between dimensions. I'm present and not present, here but not here either. To me, it's a sign that we're dealing with karma rather than lineage.

I'm in no hurry to work on the incarnations yet. I know that there is a story of a traumatic birth, and sometimes a traumatic birth is an event that affects a person's life so strongly that it can lead to difficulty with self-image. But I don't feel like that's what this is about. Maybe the issue is at the seam between this life and the soul's journey.

I ask him if he was a planned and desired pregnancy for his parents. He replies that he doesn't think so. There's something interesting about unplanned pregnancies—these are souls that choose to come, decide that it's important to come now, and create opportunities "contrary" to the wishes of the parents. It's entirely part of their soul lesson. While we talk about unwanted pregnancy and soul choice, Liron shares with me his experience of social rejection. The discourse about the traumatic pregnancy and my questions about his mother's pregnancy bring up the subject of social exclusion.

In my view, everything that comes up in the therapeutic field during a session is related to the session and to the subject. My job as a facilitator is to make connections between pieces of information that arise in the field. I asked Liron to bring representatives of social exclusion. Suddenly, the representatives of self-expression are no longer the stars of the session, but rather, representatives of rejection. It's not clear to me how rejection relates to self-expression, but I don't argue with what comes up in the field—I simply explain it. Together we choose to continue working on rejection. As rejection takes up more space in the course of our work, it becomes clear to me that the difficulty stems from karma rather than family lineage.

We place representatives of the soul and the lesson of that soul. There has been a shift in the therapeutic space which includes changes in sensation, emotion, and locations of the representatives of "expression" and "self." We place a representative of the incarnation in which the soul lesson, which is related to rejection, originated, and the story from this incarnation begins to reveal itself to us. It is the story of a boy—a young man whose village is invaded by soldiers and he feels helpless in this situation. If he stands up against them, they might kill him. The story embodies the feeling of "me against a group," and that group is dangerous to me.

We place representatives of "Past Life Me" and "The Group" to give a felt presence to the story. We make space for the fear of "Past Life Me," for his sense of helplessness in front of The Group, for the feeling that he has no tools and no ability to cope with The Group, and for the fact that dealing with them would have endangered the life of "Past Life Me." As we make more and more space for the story, fear, and helplessness, there is an emotional shift in the representatives of self-expression and rejection. They are no longer what they were at the beginning of the session. "Past Life Me" tells "Present Life Me" that he doesn't need to hold his fears within him. It was a different time, and "Present Life Me" didn't have to face this Group. Indeed, the client's representative gradually calms down, slowly loosens and, at a certain point, he feels that what happened in the previous life is no longer relevant to him and he can move forward towards his life.

Magic happens when we get to the representations of rejection and self-expression. Rejection tells us that it is connected to that incarnation and moves to stand next to all the representatives connected to that incarnation. Expression, which until now was beige (in my clinic, I work with felt fabrics as representatives) like wood flooring (which we sometimes didn't notice as it was swallowed up by the wood flooring of my clinic) takes on a new color—a brilliant greenish hue. The client doesn't notice, but the representative of "Past Life Me" is also greenish in color.

The session ends with the client standing together with his soul and self-expression in one group. He feels strong. Something had changed in his energy. New feelings of power and energy fill him.

We end the session, and I point out the change in the fabrics of self-expression and the previous incarnation. When something is missing, when there is trauma in the field, we have less energy. Once we have made space and given voice to the trauma, when we recognize what has been, healing takes place. The fact that self-expression has taken on a new energy, which is a brilliant greenish color, tells me a story of healing. That which had happened in the previous incarnation and which had been controlling the current incarnation disappeared. In its place, vitality returned and, with vitality, the ability to express oneself. The self-expression that was suppressed in the previous life, due to fear of death, was now released, and the underlying energy that had been suppressed for years could finally be expressed.

Rubik's Cube

When we do the work of going back to a past life, the incarnation we encounter has meaning to this life, to our experiences, and to the issues we are dealing with at this moment (otherwise the previous incarnation is not really interesting). Something from the previous incarnation is mixed up in or affecting the current incarnation, and the question is, what is this thing?

Karma is about, among other things, the experience of the whole. If each coin has two sides, the soul wants to experience both. I'll expand on this concept. In my eyes, karma is not a two-sided coin; it is a Rubik's cube. Imagine that completed karma is the cube, arranged so that each face is its full color. But, until then, it can be a messy cube of different colors. It takes time for all the colors to converge on one facet. It follows that if I rejected my society in a previous life, there would be a reincarnation in which I would experience a society that rejects me.

Many times, things that got stuck in the past can be released after one simple session. Karma is not about changing the story of the past, but about overcoming it. When we overcome past events, understand them, acknowledge them, and separate our past incarnation from our current one, karma can change.

Chapter 2

KARMIC CONSTELLATIONS AS A TOOL FOR CHANGING KARMA

Karmic Constellations consists of two concepts: Constellations and Working with Karma.

A Constellation is an array. The original Latin name denotes an array of stars. When you look up at the night sky, you know where the stars are. The North Star is brighter than the rest and symbolizes the direction north. The Big and Little Dipper, Orion, and more are all familiar to us. There is a physical order in the sky that keeps the stars moving and prevents them from colliding with each other and deviating from their orbit. The sky changes and the motion of the stars changes (today's North Star is probably not the same star our ancestors saw hundreds of thousands of years ago), yet all the stars in the sky remain in a certain order. No star has moved independently from its place; they continue to "sail" in the same orbit. For millions of years, Jupiter, Mars, Venus, Mercury, Earth, and others have orbited the sun. Each has its own trajectory, and yet, miraculously and in perfect balance, they do not clash with each other.

Legend has it that Bert Hellinger, the developer of Family Constellations, chose this name after looking up at the constellations in the night sky and witnessing the order that exists there. In place of a constellation of stars, each standing in its own place, he imagined working with a constellation of family members. For Bert Hellinger, the ideal or utopian family system would be organized and in order. If we lived according to this order, there would be no problems within families. But humans are not stars, and they often step out of their ideal orbit.

The differences between the sky and the family are many. In the sky, the sun does not move as it pleases. Even if it rotates and appears to move in the sky, it does so in a certain order and trajectory. Mars does not hide the sun from us, nor does Jupiter. All the stars in our solar system work in harmony and balance. Their respective solar orbits do not collide with each other; once in a while, when the moon obscures the sun, there is an eclipse, but the truth is that it is only a moment of darkness that can be predicted in advance, and when it's over, everyone returns to normal.

That's not what happens in family setups. Family setups are dynamic. We bump into each other, step on each other, and cast shadows over each other. These shadows don't last merely a few hours; sometimes they go on for a lifetime. The star system is an example of an ideal—how a family should be in its harmonious form with everyone in their right place. In life, that's not what happens. Family formations change frequently. Each extraordinary event, personal or familial—loss of a child or parent at a young age, migration or exile, transition from one culture to another, natural disaster, and other forms of loss—affects the family system. Emotions, thoughts, and behavioral patterns that were part of the family change, and new behavioral patterns enter the family system. These patterns affect the generations that follow. (The professional name for this occurrence is Intergenerational Transmission; the field that studies Intergenerational Transmission scientifically is called Epigenetics.)

Let's return for a moment to the stars. Imagine that the sun changed course and approached the earth. We would burn. Similarly, if Jupiter moved from its orbit, we could collide with it, causing great destruction and possibly even radical change to the earth's surface. If the face of the earth changes, so will we.

Family Constellations therapy is concerned with liberating a person from traumas that occurred in previous generations and disrupted the balance within the family. It restores the systemic family order so that everyone in the system feel as though they belong to the system.

The main argument of Family Constellations is that every difficulty we experience in the here and now stems from something that happened in our family history, from some harm to the family system from previous generations that we carry and according to which we conduct ourselves. When we look at the family system and get to the source of the issue, the difficulty in the here and now shifts. Sometimes it is even completely resolved.

Karmic Constellations lays a similar claim, except that instead of examining family systems, we deal with soul systems. My karmic perspective is this: When I have difficulty in this life, in the here and now of my life, the source of the difficulty is in my soul's systems, in something that happened to my soul in a previous life. When I examine the soul's systems—my past lives, soul contracts, soul lessons, vows, and so on—and find the source of my experiences today, I will be able to heal the issue in my current life.

As part of our soul lessons, our soul and karmic development, before we reach Earth and take form in a human body, we, as souls, choose the family we will be born into. We choose the family that has the highest potential to help us advance in the lessons we have chosen, the one whose story and conduct will support the path our soul seeks for itself to grow and develop.

Let's stop for a moment and take a deep breath. Yes, we chose our family or, more accurately, our soul did, but we're here with our soul. I know, sometimes it's hard to understand. Sometimes it's even downright annoying to think of it this way. Why would I choose my abusive parents? Impossible! Unfortunately, the human race, including me, is still evolving out of pain. We grow, learn, and become stronger on mental, emotional, and soul levels out of pain and suffering. It's not that we have to live in pain and suffering. Not at all. But many times, pain is the "kick in the ass" we need to change our lives for the better or to evolve.

The goal of Karmic Constellations is to find the soul system, or soul systems, that influence our here and now and release the energy of pain stored within them so that we do not have to hold onto that pain anymore. The reason we want to let go of pain is that it prevents us from seeing the lesson that has been learned in the incarnation relevant to our work. Once we let go of the pain, we can open up to seeing what we have learned and how what we have learned can serve us.

Representational Work

In representational work, we bring various elements into the therapeutic space that represent the system we are dealing with. Anything can be used as a representative: notes, nearby objects, rocks, fabrics, pillows, and more. These elements can represent people, emotions, events that have happened, past lives, soul lessons, and so forth. When I facilitate a session in a group setting, the group's participants take on this role for the client (rather than using objects) and represent the people, incarnations, souls, and so on. In a one-on-one session, different elements in the space represent these concepts for the client and they, in turn, connect to each representative and express what arises in the moment.

Representational work is about creating a connection to the quantum field, to become one with the field and with whom we represent. In simpler terms, it means becoming what we are standing in for, whether we know what that is or not. To the best of my knowledge, the first person to use representational work, at least in the Western world, was most likely the psychiatrist Jacob Moreno, who developed Psychodrama Therapy. He used representatives to make space for the client to experience events and relationships in their life through a healing lens.

Virginia Satir, a pioneering social worker, viewed families as broader than the nuclear cell, which was the common understanding at the time. She is considered the mother of Family Therapy. Satir took the idea of representatives a step further and added representatives not only of the existing family but also of the family of origin. She did so to show her clients what their children were feeling, what their family dynamics were, what they were blind to, or the influences of their family of origin. She asked people who participated in the workshops she led to come and represent her clients, who sat on stage and told their stories. The process is similar in shamanism. When the shaman embarks on a journey on behalf of his client, he goes through a soul journey as if he himself were the client.

Bert Hellinger took the work of Jacob Moreno, Virginia Satir, along with shamanic concepts a step further when he developed

Family Constellations therapy, and it is this framework I have used in developing my Karmic Constellations work.

It is important to understand that representational work is an experiential process and not a cognitive one. It's not about what you know or think, but what happens to the client in the moment, in the body—what they sense and feel.

Constellation work is not about voodoo nor about summoning energies and/or entities or the dead. By the same token, it is neither about channeling, nor is it a role-playing game of some kind. Simply put, a constellation works with the concept of stepping into someone's shoes and becoming that person. It's not about "me" thinking something about this being, nor "I" playing this being as they were described to me; rather, I become "them" and therefore feel as they do. This is one of the most unique and difficult things to explain about Constellations, yet this is what happens and it happens fantastically well.

In Family Constellations, people or objects represent family members, such as parents and grandparents, children or siblings, as well as emotions, places, and people outside the system that influence the system.

In Karmic Constellations, the subject of representation can be the previous incarnation, the person themself in the previous incarnation, and the people with whom they have contracts, shared karma, soul lessons, vows, Akashic records, and more.

The Quantum Field and Our Subconscious

The "field," as referred to in Constellations, is a spiritual term, and it contains within it the encounter of the known with the unknown, the familiar with the unfamiliar. It is the force that drives all and knows what we do not.

In the book *The Holographic Universe* Michael Talbot defines the field according to quantum theory.

He cites Einstein's statement that space and time are not separate entities, but rather, one greater whole.

Einstein called the same completeness the time–space continuum. According to Talbot, Professor David Joseph Bohm (a physicist who markedly contributed to the development of quantum and relativity theories) took this idea of Einstein's and developed it.

Bohm said that *everything* that exists in the universe is part of one continuum.

According to his theory, although all things, in their visible dimension, look and feel separate, everything is, in fact, one connected continuation of everything else. And both the hidden order and the visible order spill over into each other.

To explain this, Bohm invites us to look at the palm of our hand and at the abundant light spilling onto it while, at the same time, looking at an animal close to us. He invites us to observe and reflect on the fact that we, the light that flows upon us, and the animal are not made of the same thing—*we are the same thing*. We, the light, and the animal are one thing that cannot be separated. And this inseparable thing is something enormous that becomes all visible objects, such as atoms, oceans, and stars in space.

What Talbot is saying in this description is that if you and I are part of the whole (the same whole), I can feel you even if you are not near me and even if I do not know you. And since energy doesn't disappear but only changes form, I can be your grandmother and I can also be another incarnation of you. All is one. Constellation uses this field, this quantum wholeness, to learn from it and create change within it. Within the quantum field are our collective subconscious minds. They are part of the hidden order. This means that if we work with representatives of elements that are in our subconscious, they will leave the hidden order and become visible.

What is our subconscious? Freud, the father of psychoanalysis, used the model of an iceberg to explain the subconscious: he notes that most of what we know is above the ocean surface—"the tip of the iceberg"—and everything we don't know but controls us is found below the surface. The unconscious, where all of our unconscious memories, repressions, pains, patterns, and unconscious beliefs are stored, governs us and our lives. Today, we call it our "personal subconscious," and it is connected to other fields.

The most familiar field is the "collective unconscious," as coined by psychoanalyst Jung. The collective unconscious contains archetypal information, distinct representations that are identical throughout the world. For example, all over the globe, even before the world became global, sky was defined as masculine energy and the earth as feminine. Jung found that different symbols, such as the sun, moon, and so on, maintained the same meaning and energy in different, seemingly unrelated cultures. He found this correlation by observing the cross-cultural elements among societies located in disparate parts of the world that would have never encountered one another (slightly hard to remember, but in Jung's time there was no Internet or cellular communication all over the world as there is today). Jung coined the term "collective unconscious" based on these findings.

Between the personal subconscious and the collective unconscious is the "family subconscious"—this is our family field.

This space contains all the knowledge we have about our family lineage. As I tell my students and clients, "You don't know how much you know."

This knowledge base is enormous. It is not limited to knowledge about mom, dad, and grandparents. It can reach as far back as Adam and Eve or, in other cultures, to other spiritual ancestors. The family knowledge we hold within us is great—it is found within our genes and our emotional, energetic, and genetic intergenerational transmission. These two fields, the collective subconscious and the family subconscious, are connected to the personal subconscious; they govern and influence it.

Another field connected to the personal subconscious is the "soul field." It's a slightly different layer and yet it's present, affects our relationships, and manages a lot of our unconscious behaviors. The soul field is the field within which Karmic Constellations works. This field is connected to the hidden layers of the soul, the agreements it made before it was embodied, and everything that affects the soul in this incarnation that stems from previous lives (lessons the soul chose to learn, and more).

How do you reach all the stories that arise from these fields? How does "what I don't know that I know" become present? All this happens in the work with representatives. I check with the representatives what they feel physically and how they feel emotionally and, from the feelings and emotions, stories emerge. Clients' perceptions such as: "My mother is not a nice woman" are less relevant to the work of the Karmic Constellations. What is relevant to constellation work is what emerges from the body— that's what I work with. Many times visions, images, and even memories arise out of the sensations and emotions of a session.

In one of the Karmic Constellations sessions I facilitated, the client discussed a representative of a previous life. She didn't see anything, just felt physical sensations: "I'm uncomfortable in my stomach," she told me. When I asked her to stay a little longer with the discomfort in her stomach, an inner experience of being a teenager came up. I asked her to stay with that feeling and pay attention to what was buried inside it. As she stayed with the teenager, the discomfort grew and a whole story began to emerge of a girl who was murdered suddenly (presumably stabbed in the back). Once the story revealed itself in the field, the client felt calm and the discomfort disappeared.

Staying with the representation, and the sometimes uncomfortable experience it brings up, initiates a person into a hidden layer of being: the soul subconscious. This allows content to move from the subconscious, which is the hidden layer, to the conscious, which is the visible layer. Once the story is expressed, clients tend to feel quite good. The hidden layer ceases to hold weight and govern patterns of behavior, thought, and conduct. As a result, the trauma is released from the subconscious and enables a new life experience.

Acknowledging What Is

One of the principles of Constellations is "acknowledging what is." Acknowledging what is speaks to making space for that which has been hidden. It is the act of moving from darkness into light. This can refer to a secret or an emotion that has not been expressed.

As human beings, we constantly choose what to express and what not to; we reinforce a thought or belief and repress another. We express ourselves and silence those voices or thoughts within us we deem incompatible with our environment, or that our environment has let us know is impermissible and will be punished.

Acknowledging *what is* makes it possible to recognize all that has been silenced within us and to give it space. The very acknowledgment of *what was* brings healing. We are not seeking to heal the previous incarnation (at least I am not). We seek to make room for repressed voices, unspoken beliefs, and subconscious thoughts. We aim to give voice to that which was forbidden. When the forbidden to be said is said, relief is created in the field. Change occurs.

Recognition permits pain and trauma from previous lives to rise to the surface. It releases energies from our soul subconscious that control us often subliminally. This process makes it possible to change our behavior in the current incarnation. That is, karma can be changed or released.

The true healing does not come from changing what happened or creating a corrective experience. It emerges by providing space for words, experiences, sensations, desires, fears, and more, which had no place, did not receive expression, and wandered with the soul from incarnation to reincarnation, thereby influencing its conduct. When we make room for all these, the soul is released and an opening for change is created.

Changing Reality in One Session

When Bert Hellinger developed Family Constellations, he argued that it takes two years for the constellations process to take shape in a person's life. Since then much has changed, and constellations facilitators around the world lead constellations sessions more often than every two years. Still, in my opinion, when it comes to addressing a specific issue, often one session is enough and there's no need for several sessions or a process.

Imagine a lake with still water. The view of the surrounding trees and mountains is copied onto the lake's surface in a perfect mirror image. That which is outside seems to be inside, and it's difficult to discern between reality and reflection. Now imagine a concrete block weighing one ton gets thrown into the center of the lake. Waves and ripples are created and these waves and ripples change the reflection completely, erasing parts and distorting others. It will take time for the lake to return to stillness, relax, and be part of the whole once again. The process can range from a few moments to a few days, depending on the size of the lake and its depth. This is exactly what happens in a constellation session. The ripples of the session affect our lives but often take their time.

There are sessions that are immediately followed by movement and change in life, as shared with me by one of the clients who came in to deal with obsessive thoughts she had about her ex-partner who she broke up with about twenty years prior and without whom she experienced a full and complete life. She and I met for one session that dealt with life on another planet and her soul's arrival on Earth and, within a month, after years of obsessive thoughts, she stopped thinking about him. On the other hand, there are issues that require patience. We, or our lives, are not ready yet and change happens slowly.

That which the soul is not prepared for, or contradicts the soul's lesson, will not happen. It doesn't matter how many sessions or treatment methods we do. Moreover, that which corresponds to the soul's lesson, but not to the person's timeline, will happen when it is right for both the soul and the person. In addition, Karmic Constellations works with origins. It deals with that which created the lesson or contract. Life is viewed as a symptom—an effect. For example, if you're struggling financially, this is a result of something that happened in a past life. When we discover the source, the financial struggle will change here and now, in the current incarnation.

Are there several origins or incarnations for the same issue? Possibly. At the same time, as I said earlier, it's like a snowball rolling from the top of a mountain. As it descends the mountain, it gains momentum and grows. In Karmic Constellations we say that if we reach the moment when the snowball was formed and we can change it, then we will change its unfolding, momentum, and size, or at least stop it before it runs us down at the base of the mountain. Therefore, a Karmic Constellation is defined as a one-time encounter, not a process. I am an emotionally based therapist and was trained to work with people in emotional work. Albeit for a relatively short period of time, I am trained in a process-oriented manner. However, this is not the case in constellation. A Karmic Constellation is a one-time session.

This is what Constellations does for a person—it changes their soul and their life. Unlike regular therapy, in which the therapist asks the person about their life in depth, Constellations does not require that. I spend 5 to 10 minutes questioning the client and, in this questioning, what I want to discover is what the person in front of me wants to change in their life. Many times statements like, "I want to change my soul's contract with my mom," or "I feel stuck in business," or "I can't make friends," are enough for me to set up a constellation session. Too much information can block me and create paradigms within me. When working with a constellation, the facilitator holds the container and space and provides direction, but the real therapist—the one from whom the information comes—is the field.

Karmic Constellation in Service of Change

Our current incarnation aims to enable us to balance or complete the karma we bring from previous lives: to come to terms with souls we have hurt in previous lives or to have new experiences. Most of the people we meet in our lives, especially our family and friends, are related to our karma. When there is pain in these connections, our goal is to discover the source of the pain and create change within it. Pain is found in our soul lessons, in our contracts, in our energetic memories, and it is expressed in our lives, in our patterns and behaviors, and in the patterns and behaviors of our environment.

Corinne's Story

Corinne arrived after doing many treatments, including several Family Constellations, and she still hadn't experienced change in the issue of her concern, social rejection. She felt stuck. She felt unable to socialize and constantly experienced a sense of rejection from friends and society at large.

We placed representatives for her, her soul, rejection, and society. The process began. Her feelings towards the representations of society weren't easy, neither for her nor for her soul. Nor did society seem to care for her and her soul, just as she has experienced in her reality.

I was interested to find out what the hidden story was—its origin—and why she had a hard time with society and society had a hard time with her. I brought out a representation of her soul contract followed by a representation of the previous incarnation. A lot of pain came up.

When she stood in for the representative of the past life, I asked her to bring a representation of who she was in this life. She stood in for the representative of "Past Life Me" and noticed what came up. (When I ask people to stand in for a representation and ask, "What comes up for you?" I mainly emphasize feelings and sensations, as well as various images that arise in the minds of the representatives.) In her mind's eye, she saw an image of herself being dragged by her hair. I asked her to bring a representation of this person who was dragging her. She brought a representation and stood on it. A sense of superiority and of "she belongs to me" arose from the representation. Simultaneously, there was a fear and unwillingness to agree with that person's sense of ownership as the representative for "Past Life Me."

At this stage of the constellation I aim to create greater clarity for myself and the client regarding the subject. At such moments, I often ask the participants in the constellation to say sentences. The purpose of the sentences is to create clarity as well as to bring feelings of well-being and recognition of "what is" into the session.

Standing in for the man from the previous life, I asked her to say to the representation of "Past Life Me," "You are mine according to the laws of the society." When she said it as the representative, it felt right to her. That's exactly what he felt towards her.

She then stood in for "Past Life Me" and disagreed with his statement. I instructed her to reply, "I reject you and the laws of society." As a representation of "Past Life Me," it felt right to her. When there is a society, and it has laws, and we reject the laws of this society, we are actually rejecting the society. And that's what her "Past Life Me" did—reject society.

Many times, when we act intensely about a certain subject (justified/unjustified is a human perception), the soul will choose to manifest the opposite experience. I call this "compensation" or "completion." The desire is to complete the knowledge, to experience both sides of the coin. We saw through Karmic Constellations that, in the previous incarnation, Corinne rejected society and, in the current incarnation, she was born to a society that rejected her. Corinne's lesson was actually a new experience. The soul chose to experience something it hadn't before, and which stemmed from a previous life in which the opposite had happened.

Becca's Story

Becca's story beautifully illustrates how a collection of experiences from past lives directs our lives in this incarnation and how we can be released in order to create something new. Becca's story:

"I want more money in my life," she tells me.

"Well, let's get to work," I reply, and we begin. She places representations of:

- Me
- My Soul
- Money

I want to see what happens in the field. Do I need to bring a representation for "my lesson with money"? How about a representation for "More Money in My Life"? I don't know and am waiting to see what comes from the representatives. She stands on the fabric representing money. A story emerges. She envisions an angry mob with knives and sticks that she wants to cross to reach beyond it, but she can't get through. She's scared.

We continue the session, and the crowd, the angry mob, appears again and again in her mind's eye. I instruct her to bring representations of the crowd and of what lies beyond the crowd. She places the representatives and stands in for Money again. The crowd suddenly becomes friendly, and she can be with them.

Many times in a constellation, representations can start as a particular subject and then become something else. In this case, money has become Becca-from-a-Previous-Life (this is a common phenomenon in representation work. A representative begins as something specific and changes its energy and essence into something else. For example, from money to "Me from a Previous Life" or from "Me in This Life" to "Me from a Previous Life").

From the work with the representatives and the knowledge Becca brought from sessions in other therapeutic modalities, I realized that Becca has a pattern that has been repeated in more than one incarnation—she "chases" a certain goal but dies along the way. This understanding made me ask Becca to place a representative of this pattern.

The representation of the pattern was next to Becca. We saw that the soul wanted to ignore it—to take Becca and move ahead. Becca's soul's solution to this pattern until now had been to ignore the pattern, but that wasn't working out so well for her because the pattern continued to disturb her and create stagnation in her life. Therefore, we made space for this understanding and also for the soul's desire to ignore it. When Becca stood in for the pattern, she felt that it didn't belong to anyone but affected everyone. It was collateral damage that hurt everyone.

After that, she stood in for the representation of herself and felt that she could move forward to the crowd and also to that which is beyond the crowd. She moved, crossed the crowd, and reached what was beyond. She saw trees. She was still afraid. She stood in for the representation of her soul, and her soul approached and stood behind her to support her.

Since our subject was money, but money became Becca in a previous incarnation, I brought a new representative for money in this incarnation. He, too, stood behind Becca's representative in support. There was still a connection between Becca's representative and "what's beyond the crowd." In my experience as a facilitator, "what's beyond the crowd" is like the promised land to Moses. You see it, but something or someone prevents you from reaching it. That's exactly what happened in Becca's previous lives—there were goals, but over and over again she died or was killed and couldn't achieve them.

It's an accumulated energy. When we have accumulated energy in karma, two things happen:

1 We come back here to fix it.
2 It's very difficult to correct because the pattern is so familiar that we tend to recycle it over and over again.

Creating change requires recognizing what happened and aligning with a new purpose. Instead of chasing the Promised Land, we could set more feasible goals. So we brought representatives of relevant goals for this incarnation. Instead of chasing goals from the past, we shifted the energy to relevant goals. Now the soul, money in this incarnation, and the goals of this incarnation all stood in support of Becca.

Until the session, every time Becca set goals for herself she failed to achieve them, but now Becca felt capable of creating goals and taking an easy approach to her mission, moving forward in her life, achieving goals, and earning money. The new goals will be accurate to this incarnation, not only in their labels but also in Becca's experience.

Changing Karma—In Practice

Over the course of this chapter we saw how situations of years of stagnation were released and change was created. This is what I call "karmic change." Instead of getting stuck in familiar patterns, we allow the new to manifest. Many times we bring with us a certain energy from past lives. Sometimes it's an empowering energy that pushes us forward, and other times it's an impeding energy.

As we saw in Becca's session, we don't know that this energy is emanating from previous lives and tend to repeat the cycle as if we were experiencing it for the first time, thus intensifying the energy and also remaining stuck in the same place and experience as the last incarnation.

In Becca's case, the energy from previous lives was represented by money. But it can be anything. These can be relationships, career, parenting, partnerships, and more. Once the thing (in this case, money) acquires its true essence—that is, it clearly traces back to a previous incarnation—it is much easier to separate the previous incarnation from the current incarnation and produce new energy.

This is what we did in Corinne's session. We saw what happened in the past, experienced the energy it brought to this incarnation, and we separated the incarnations. What has been, has been; now something new can begin.

We are the sum of our past. Who we are today is the result of everything we've been through in our lives, current and past.

But the opposite is also true. We have the ability to take the traumas, vows, promises, and stagnation from the past and, instead of repeating them, to heal, recognize, and understand them. When this happens, they become life experience, which can move us forward and support us. Furthermore, observing the previous life and understanding it allows us to learn new things, break out of patterns, complete the lesson, and release karma related to that subject.

Chapter 3

WORKING WITH
THE SOUL

"My soul was finally realizing its true magnificence! And, in doing so, it was expanding beyond my body and this physical world. It extended further and further outward until it encompassed not only this existence, but continued to expand into another realm that was beyond this time and space, and at the same time included it."[3]

In this quote by Anita Moorjani, one can find an accurate and concise description of the soul. The soul is energy. It is boundless and timeless. In our perception, the soul is within us and, therefore, we frame it within the boundaries of our body. In fact, it is not. The soul has no boundaries of time and space.

In the process of incarnation, part of the soul is reduced and enters the person's body, but in its essence, the soul remains infinite.

This is what The Group told me about the soul:

---

3 Anita Moorjani, *Dying to Be Me: My Journey from Cancer, to Near Death, to True Healing.* Carlsbad, CA: Hay House, 2012.

Beloved, beloved, beloveds, sounds, unique and delicate
infinite geometry, each of you, like a snowflake, is made of
a wonderful jigsaw puzzle of color, sound, and geometry.
Oh, dear ones, you are holy, a soul is a holy thing. If only
you knew how profoundly in His image you are. You are
He, or She or They, no matter the terminology, you are
The Being Itself and, as such, you are sanctified. That is the
soul; the soul is one. You are all one; you are all The One.

Not only did you not come from dust and to dust you
will not return, even though your body is dust, but in your
essence, you came from the Light, the Source, the Creation,
the Infinite Creator; you are the Love. You are God's love
for His children, your love for yourselves; you are the love
of this sphere and the love of humanity. If only you knew
how much you are loved, how much you are love. If only
you would listen to the notes that make up the essence of
who you are, or look at the very geometry you are built
of. We are not referring to the shape or energy of the
Merkaba but to something far beyond that. Every being,
every soul, every person is made up of an infinite number
of geometries, sounds, and colors. When spirit becomes
solid, it becomes solid through shapes, colors, and the
sound of music, the notes. This is the clearest explanation
of what a soul is, even if it's not at all clear. You are made of
notes, thin silver threads that create the unique snowflake
that is you. Each such flake was lovingly carved by God
Himself and Herself. Gender is a human construct; it is not
the language of love.

Each of you was created in love and is love and one
day will return to love. One of the soul's goals is to discover

this love, within itself and in the world. You are dear ones, the infinite Light, the essence of the soul—Light, Love, Godliness. The purpose of reincarnation is to uncover in matter the fact that you are Light, Love, God. This is our answer to what the soul is. We are The Group.

— The Group

I have a slightly more mundane perspective:

The soul, as I see it, is like an entity created by and from creation itself. It descends to Earth, to the human body, in order to have additional experiences that will aid its development and growth. The soul is eternal and, during its journey on Earth, it has experienced everything: emotions, sensations, actions, patterns of behavior. It has been a man, and it has been a woman. It was married, and it was single. It was rich and poor. It was a murderer and the murdered. It has experienced and aims to experience as much of the human world as possible in order to increase its knowledge of Self and the world.

Humanity changes and, therefore, every time the soul descends to reincarnate in a body, it experiences things differently. For example, the concept of love and relationships has changed over the years and, in light of the cultures that have come and gone in our world, from periods when there was no monogamy and everyone lived together in one tribe, to today, when most live in their own homes with a partner or alone. Even now, in our today, love and relationships are perceived radically differently in different parts of the world. A soul that wants to explore, for example, the concept of femininity, can choose in each incarnation to come to a different country and culture, once in England, once in the United States, once in Africa, once in Japan and, each time, she will have a different and new experience. The disparity between the experiences of different cultures is what moves the soul through another stage of its development.

We Are Not Our Souls

Although we have a tendency to identify and think of ourselves as one with our soul, we are not our souls. The concept of "Self" is an elusive concept. What defines my "Self"? Being a woman? A mother? Being my parents' daughter? How about being a business owner? Or maybe neither? Most of us stick to labels because it's easier for us to recognize and find ourselves in categories. It helps us feel that there is order and flow within ourselves and in the world. Our perception of the "Self" is made up of many layers, parts, and shades.

This concept of "Self" is joined by our perception of the soul. Is the soul a part of us? How does it affect us? Is it us or are we the soul? Since we cannot see the soul and we do not know its identity nor its energy, we tend to define it as part of our "Self" or the entirety of our "Self." This reminds me of a baby who doesn't understand that they are a separate entity from their mother until they learn to crawl. The crawling physically separates them from their mother, and they discover that they and their mother are not one.

The soul is in our body, but the soul is not our whole body (just as the brain is not our whole body). While it is within us, it also exists in the world of souls. A soul is not a linear thing; it is energy and frequency. In his book *The Journey of Souls*, Dr. Michael Newton says he learnt that there are differences between the identity of the soul and what the human body expresses. He cites as an example, souls that choose bodies that act differently than the fixed self of the soul, like a calm soul that chooses a hyperactive body, or an active soul that chooses a delicate and fragile body.

For many years I found it difficult to understand the concept that the soul is not me. In my perception, my body was "me" and, therefore, my soul was also "me." I couldn't understand the separation between the "self," "body," and "soul." My desires expressed the will of my soul and there was a clear shared identity between them, so the choices and actions I had made in my life were naturally correlated with the will of my soul. I did not understand, nor could I handle the concept of separation between my "self," my "soul," and my "body."

One day I met a medium who told me I was running too fast; that my soul was tired of the race and wanted me to slow down. This was the first time I had an experience of "splitting." Apparently, my soul is not me, and there are things I do that are incompatible with my soul. After meeting this medium, the message that my soul and I were not in alignment was repeated to me several times in different ways, always from outside sources. Someone else would repeat the information and it became a mental understanding, but not an inner experience that could spur me into action.

My encounter with Family Constellations and the work of representation taught me that everything has a representative and a voice. The "Self" is not one thing, but many things. For example, when I published a parenting guidebook, *The Alchemy of Parenthood*, I used a representation for the book and found that there were things the book wanted/needed and I did not. The book wanted a launch; I didn't.

Many times in representation work, I will break down the subject into as many representatives as possible in order to listen to each voice. When a person comes to a Constellations session and the subject is low self-esteem, I will place four representations: a representative of the client, of the esteem, of the self, and of the "low." I will break down the phrase "self-esteem" into two. And even though there is already a "Self" in a session, we often find that between "I" (the client) and "self," there can be a great deal of variation.

This realization ignited a curiosity in me about realms beyond family or business, and so began my exploration of karmic work. I placed a representation of myself and a representation of my soul and, to my surprise, discovered two different worlds. For the first time, I experienced first-hand inside myself that my soul and self are not the same, that our needs and desires are slightly different and, especially striking, that the quality of my soul is completely different from my person. While I have a tendency to live in the fast lane, my soul actually moves somewhat slower. It's not rushing anywhere. This experience of a gap between my soul and my "Self" has repeated several times and continues to show up to this day. Not everything I do is aligned with my soul's needs and desires, even if my intuition told me to do it. Not every craving or desire of mine is in line with the soul. Like me, my clients and students also experience the gap between the "Self" and the soul.

"Me" and "My Soul"

When we place a representation of the soul and a representation of "me" we often experience a difference, as I did when I placed representatives of myself and my soul and felt completely divergent feelings and sensations. We have a relationship with our soul and sometimes it's quite complex. I've led sessions in which the soul wanted no contact with the client, the "self," as well as sessions in which the client, the "self," did not want contact with the soul.

This state of division between elements that express our whole essence is unhealthy. Think about your right hand. What would happen if it suddenly doesn't want you? What if it suddenly decides that it doesn't like you? It doesn't want to do what you want it to do. Or, alternatively, what if you suddenly don't like your right hand and don't want it to be a part of you?

This analogy is similar to our relationship with the soul. We are together, we are one, but equally each has its own consciousness, and these minds do not always get along.

Exercise
Tuning In to the Energies

Take a piece of notepaper and write your name on it. Now get another note and write "My Soul" on it. Put your hand on the note with your name written on it. What are the sensations? What emotions arise in you? What happens when you look at the note that says "My Soul"? What feelings and sensations are rising in you now?

Take your hand off the note with your name on it and put your hand on the note that says "My Soul." What are the feelings now? Are they the same as the feelings you had when your hand was on the note with your name? Are the sensations different?

What happens when you have your hand on "My Soul" and look at the note with your name written on it? What feelings and sensations arise in you? Do you feel pleasant, uncomfortable, neutral?

Take your hand off the note.

First of all, this is representation work.

Secondly, did you experience any differences between the notes? Were the sensations in your body unique to each note/identity?

They may have been the same, and you may not have sensed or felt anything. This is completely natural.

Take another note and write down a topic that concerns you. Any topic: livelihood, abundance, your relationship with your parents, relationships, self-esteem, and so on. There are no bounds to the issues that concern us.

Write down only one topic on the note.

Now place your hands on the note that says your name. Are the sensations the same as before, or has something changed? When your hand is on the note, what happens to you when you look at your soul? Are the sensations the same as before or have they changed? And what happens to you when you look at the note with the topic? Which feelings have changed?

Now put your hand on the note of "My Soul." What happens to your feelings and sensations now? Are they the same as before or has something changed? What's changed?

Put your hand on the note with your name, what happens to you now? What feelings and sensations arise in you? Are they similar or different than the ones you had before? And when you look at the topic in question that you wrote about, what happens?

This small exercise provides a wonderful illustration of how often our soul and "Self" experience things differently. Bringing the soul closer to the "Self" and vice versa is part of the healing process and changing our reality in the physical body. We must create a connection between the two. The more connected we are to our soul, the more connected we are to our being and the fuller our experience of life.

From Linear to Infinite

As humans we are very linear creatures. We experience life in past–present–future. Yesterday–today–tomorrow. One thing precedes the next. Night comes after day, and day after night. The human perception of time is linear and, through it, we observe the world.

We count seven days a week when, in truth, counting days is a figment of man's imagination and is only a way to define and manage time so as to define a past and future. By defining time we define many things. We define ages, periods, cultural characteristics, and more.

Our brains, and even our minds, often find it easier to work with the linear. It is much easier for us to look at something linearly than abstractly. Since ancient times mankind has sought to define time. Initially we did so by looking at the moon. The waxing and waning of the moon was the first way to mark time. This was followed by tracking seasons and defining them as such. The concept of time gives us a sense of certainty. We have a hard time with uncertainty and similar difficulty with abstract ideas or concepts. We search for the concrete, the illustrative. Abstract concepts are difficult at best, incomprehensible at worst.

The soul is an abstract concept. By virtue of being eternal it is a nonlinear concept. And by virtue of being an abstract concept, it is difficult for us to understand and contain it. It has no limits—no limits of body, nor of time or space. It does not experience yesterday–today–tomorrow and is not a tangible being. Our soul is here, in our physical body, and also in the world of souls. It lives on several planes simultaneously.

Man perceives life in a linear or three-dimensional way. The soul, however, does not. For the soul, everything happens now, simultaneously. Our previous incarnation is happening now. In fact, all of our past incarnations are happening now and are having an impact now. We can, therefore, influence them now, in this incarnation.

One of my clearest spontaneous memories of my past life is World War I in England. I have a memory of accompanying my fiancé to the train station and parting from him there as he was on his way to war with a promise that when he returned we would marry. He never returned, and I, in that incarnation, never married. Although the woman I was in 1918 passed away, her soul lives on.

In her book *Dying to Be Me*, Anita Moorjani describes her experience with space/time: "Time felt different in that realm, too, and I felt all moments at once. I was aware of everything that pertained to me—past, present, and future—simultaneously. I became conscious of what seemed to be simultaneous lives playing out."[4]

Since the soul field is not linear, the influence of past lives is also not linear. It is not always what happened in the previous incarnation that affects the current incarnation. Sometimes the defining influence will come from something that happened 20 incarnations and 2,000 years ago.

---

4 Anita Moorjani. *Dying to Be Me*. Carlsbad, CA: Hay House, 2012.

Why Incarnate?

"A life is never useless. Each soul that came down to Earth is here for a reason."[5]

When the soul incarnates in the body, it has an objective. Often it has several objectives. Some of the goals are personal—to experience joy, to cope with difficulties in relationships, parenting, to practice love—and some are collective or even for humanity: to incite change in human consciousness, to amend the legal system, change welfare institutions, and more.

The soul chooses its life. It chooses to have different and varied experiences with the aim of enriching its world of practical knowledge and strengthening its soul core. The soul is part of a collective, and one of its goals is to promote the development of consciousness in humanity.

In principle, the goal of the soul is to grow and heal past traumas. Hence, every incarnation has a purpose. It is a general purpose, in the sense that it is aimed at the growth of the soul and, additionally, it contains within it specific goals, such as refining the soul, connecting to human emotion, expanding specific knowledge: mastering music or acquiring new skills such as self-regulation.

The way the soul fulfills its goals is by choosing a lineage to be born into, places to live, and people it will meet throughout its life. Because the soul is eternal, it has a wealth of knowledge and experience. Some of this wealth affects our lives now, for better or worse.

Apart from the goals, which are "forgotten" as soon as we are born, the soul carries with it memories and traumas from past

---

5 Paulo Coelho, *Manuscript Found in Accra*. Reprint edition. New York, NY: Vintage, 2013.

lives. When it reaches the current incarnation, there are people, places, and things that remind it of the previous lives it experienced, and these memories surface and influence our behavior in this incarnation, even though we, as human beings, were not alive then and the memories reflect different times, a different country, and even a different gender.

Marcia's Story

Marcia came to me because she was searching for a romantic relationship. After her previous relationship ended, she felt a great loss and became depressed. It took her five years to get over it. She began looking for a relationship but couldn't find one. She tried various forms of treatment but nothing changed in her life, so she turned to Karmic Constellations.

In the session we looked for the source of the difficulty she was experiencing today. We reached a previous incarnation in which there was a great love between the husband and his wife, but the wife was taken by warriors and murdered. The pain was profound and, moreover, a vow had been made by the wife not to leave her husband. That is, she would stay with him, emotionally and energetically, even after her death.

We realized that Marcia still contained the energy of the pain from this past life, and also the energy of the vow. All of this made her feel as if her life was over when her previous relationship ended. As part of the session, we released the pain from the previous life, the attachment to it, and also the vow. Marcia's sensations changed from heaviness and great pain in the chest to a sense of well-being and regulated breathing.

Marcia's story illustrates the impact of past lives on the present.

The purpose of Karmic Constellations is to release the energetic attachments we carry with us from previous incarnations.

When we experience difficulty in a certain area of our lives, whether it is in relationships, livelihood, parenting, or any other arena, we can ascertain that there is a soul story there. In Karmic Constellations, we ask questions like: "What is in my soul's journey that requires me to learn and practice this subject? What influenced my soul to choose this lesson? What is the source of this particular soul journey or difficulty?"

We bring a representation of the soul lesson and examine in which incarnation it was created and what created it. The incarnation in which the lesson was created is considered the source. There, according to the Karmic Constellations lens, the lesson and the journey of learning and practice of the subject began.

The purpose of soul work in Karmic Constellations is to release the effects of past lives and allow the energy that was stuck there to dissolve and liberate us in the here and now. Once we reach the source incarnation and understand what happened, how it affects us, and the implications, we can free ourselves from this incarnation. When this happens, our soul can stop carrying the guilt/shame/trauma or anything else it carries within it that affects it and us.

This creates a change in the current incarnation. The previous incarnation is no longer a burden or hindrance to the current one and ceases to affect us. Moreover, in every incarnation, there is an abundance of life experience, knowledge, lessons, and keys to our advancement.

Trauma is like a screen. It masks our eyes from seeing what we have learned so that the incarnation and its richness become inaccessible to us. When we see the trauma and cleanse the painful energy stored in the previous life, its richness, life experience, and positive teachings are revealed to us and can benefit us in this incarnation.

Orit's Story

Orit came to me after the second COVID-19 pandemic lockdown. Something was unsettled within her. It had to do with the vaccination policy and the anxiety of those around her. She had a hard time accepting what was happening in the world, and it affected her. As a therapist, the lockdowns affected her financially, but they were impacting her mentally as well; something in her was unsettled. She wanted to feel protected and remain untouched by everything that was happening around her, to regain control of her path and chart her own trajectory.

We did a session and connected to a previous incarnation. In that incarnation, Orit was an important general who had trampled villages without compunction and was involved in dozens of cases of looting and rape. This was not something Orit wanted to connect with at all. But that general was a great general for one reason: he was an excellent strategist. He didn't just trample villages and destroy them; he did what he did with forethought, not out of reflex or rage.

That's what Orit wanted to connect with—the ability to build a strategy for herself that would serve her in these uncertain times. After we processed his ruthless, murderous character and understood it was the soul's choice in that incarnation, Orit could access his strategic prowess. This created peace within Orit. When she returned to her practice, she felt a change in herself. The session was a turning point for Orit and connected her deeply to her essence, which expressed itself in her personal life as well as her therapeutic practice.

One of the interesting things that happens when you read the books of Dr. Michael Newton and Dr. Brian L. Weiss is that you realize the soul is not only light and love but also contains greater complexities. I see this in Karmic Constellations work with representations. Often when people represent souls, the experience is one of victimization, guilt, pain, and other worldly human emotions.

How can this be? How is it possible that the representation of the soul speaks in a mundane and practical way? In Constellations parlance, we call this "entanglement." Entanglement is a way in which the field tells us that there is a story here that has to do with other lives, that there is an open wound here from another story, and that there is now some willingness on the part of the soul to heal that open wound and move forward, delivering healing to the person and the soul. By bringing up past lives and the stories that were present then, we release the entanglement and enable energies to regroup.

It is important to note that Karmic Constellations is not concerned with healing traumas from a previous life nor with creating corrective experiences. The very ability to connect to the previous life, to see the trauma, to name it, and to recognize that it is connected to another era is what creates healing in the current incarnation.

Although on a soul level there is no time, time continues to exist in the human experience. Consequently, past lives belong to the past. They already happened. What remains in the energy of the soul is the pain, guilt, and shame associated with that experience. The very recognition of these feelings dissolves them. The recognition of past actions and the acknowledgment that they are irrelevant to our present, diminishes and can even completely eliminate their energetic hold.

Chapter 4

SOUL AGREEMENTS AND SHARED KARMA

The Soul Family as an Assistant to the Soul's Evolutionary Journey

We are not alone here. We are not alone in our journey across this planet. We have partners. Our parents, nuclear family, extended family, classmates, spouses, children, teachers, colleagues, bosses, employees, the taxi and bus drivers, neighbors, the usher at the entrance to the movies—we are all connected.

Just as we are part of a family in this world, we are part of a soul family in the world of souls. Our soul family has always been with us. It is part of our soul's journey and reincarnates with us in many different lives. Each lifetime our soul family takes on new roles and new ways to help each other. The roles can be parents and children, good friends, business partners, spouses, uncles and aunts, and so on.

Each soul descends into the world to experience growth and development through human experiences. As the soul descends, so do the souls of its soul family. Each soul experiences events for its own pleasure and in order to initiate the processes it has sought to go through. Much of it will be experienced alongside and through its soul family. I don't know how many souls are in our soul family. Some will say 15 and others thousands or even tens of thousands. I do know that we have common contracts for learning and development together with many members of our soul family.

In his book *The Journey Home*, Lee Carroll tells the story of Michael Thomas, who is on a journey of personal development. At one point, Michael Thomas arrives at a house, where he is introduced to his soul family. The purpose of the meeting is to show him soul contracts; to show him that everyone in his life, including those who hurt him in the past or in his childhood, are all part of his soul family. They are part of the contracts and lessons he has chosen in his life, and they are all there out of love. Among other things, he meets Shirley, the love of his life, who left him and whom he defined as the one who ruined his life. Here's what Shirley tells him:

> Michael Thomas, I am Reenuei . . . I am your family [in other words, she's telling Michael that she's a part of his soul family], and I love you dearly! I am Shirley, as you know me in this life. Before that I was Fred, your brother in the last century. Before I was Fred, I was Cynthia, your wife before that. Michael Thomas of Pure Intent, we have a contract, and the energy of it is called karma. We had planned together to meet again in this life, and we did. You and I have completed something we both started centuries ago, and we did it well. We agreed to generate feelings in you that would bring you to this crossroads in life. It is my gift to you, and yours to me. We did it together![6]

---

6   Lee Caroll, *The Journey Home, A Kryon Parable: The Story of Michael Thomas and the Seven Angels.* Carlsbad, CA: Hay House, 1997.

What Is a Soul Contract?

Imagine yourself going to rent an apartment. You make an appointment with the landlord and meet there. You look around and, if you like it, you'll sign a contract with the landlord. The main things you sign for are the payment of rent and the condition of the apartment as it appeared to you during the tour. Only after you sign the contract can you move into the apartment.

The contract you signed is a legal contract in every respect. What's not in the contract? You won't know from this lease whether your landlord, who seems nice, is indeed nice. He could be a troublesome landlord who harasses you every other day. You also won't know from the contract that the refrigerator, which seems normal to you, frequently breaks down and that the Wi-Fi signal in the apartment is poor and impossible to fix. All these unexpected realities affect you and your quality of life at least as much as the place itself.

This is a good metaphor for the soul contract in my opinion. We sign soul contracts before we even incarnate in the body. We seal it, soul to soul. We don't really know how we'll feel inside our physical bodies and how we'll receive our experience on this planet. Like the fridge and the Wi-Fi, things seem a certain way to us as souls, and sometimes, when we manifest in the body, they look and feel differently to us.

A soul contract is a connection between souls, made in the world of souls, with the aim of evolving, developing, learning, and overcoming obstacles we weren't able to in previous lives. Despite the name "contract," which creates the connotation of something legal, soul contracts are not required to be honored—there are no clauses nor an obligation to succeed in fulfilling them (if there are indeed clauses in the contract).

There are no courts to pass sentence for breach of contract or non-compliance.

A soul contract is an act of love in which two souls meet in the world of souls and *choose* to help each other. But don't let the word "choose" confuse you. Just as we choose to experience love, satisfaction, happiness, connection, we may absolutely choose to undergo less pleasant experiences, such as difficulty, violence, bullying, abandonment, and so forth. We may also choose to be the one who beats, bullies, abandons, or murders. It takes two to tango. This is the dance that souls do before they even descend to Earth.

There is a difference between a soul's choice and human's choice. I would never tell a battered woman that she chose to experience violence. If and when she goes through a process and sees that her soul has chosen it, then she will be able to free herself from wherever she is. The soul's choice is very different from human choice. Our human choices are often built on unconscious paths related to our subconscious mind and our soul's choices. No one would deliberately and ignorantly choose to be beaten, murdered, humiliated, or raped. Therefore, when a client comes to me who is experiencing difficulty, I will not tell them that they chose it. I'll let the "field" show them what they need to see. It is this vision, this understanding, if and when it arises, that will create change within them and their life.

Danny is a medium. He came to me to work on his relationship with his children. While he was with me, he told me that since he was two years old he knew that he hadn't come here voluntarily. The guidance had forced him to descend and be born to his parents. He can't stand his parents.

When we started doing Karmic Constellations, we placed a representation of his guidance. When he stood in for the representation of himself, in front of the representations of his guides, suddenly he saw something. When I asked him what it was, he told me that he saw that he did choose to come here, that his spiritual guides accompanied him through the birth canal, and that no one forced him to come and be born to these parents. For over thirty years, Danny told himself a story that supported his sense of victimhood towards his mother. An encounter with the guidance, through Karmic Constellations, allowed him to see his soul's choice.

Why should we choose parents we are not happy with? There are lots of reasons. In fact, there are as many reasons as there are children that are unhappy with their parents, and each is its own story. In order to understand these choices, one must understand that there is a divide between the world of souls and the physical world, and the gap can be enormous.

Souls are energy; they do not experience the physical body. If someone gives us a kiss on the cheek, we'll feel all sorts of things. It can be pleasant or unpleasant. It can be wet or piercing or warm. And the person giving the kiss will also sense the cheek, be it warm or cold, with or without stubble, pleasant or unpleasant. Our body responds to another body. But if we blow a kiss in the air or give a kiss to the air, we won't feel anything, and neither will the air. The body is what makes the experience real. The air got a kiss, but it wasn't tangible, whereas when we get a kiss on our physical body, it has a real feeling. If we think of air as a metaphor for our soul, we can imagine for a moment that the air can think to itself that getting kisses is really fun and, therefore, it will choose to become a physical body that has skin and senses. Then it will get a kiss. Now the experience of this kiss will be subjective.

Like air, when the soul chooses abusive parents, it understands that the journey will be tough, but it has no way of estimating how difficult it will actually be when it incarnates into a human body. When souls choose life, they know that life may not be simple, but they do not fully internalize the concept of "not simple" or the intensity of pain, because they are energetic bodies rather than sensory beings. The pain and complexity of life are experienced in the body, on this planet, and not in the world of souls. Matter and physicality are what promote our soul development. There is no pain in the world of souls.

When a soul "falls" in the world of souls (if it is at all possible to fall when we are an amorphous entity with no tangible form), it senses nothing. When we fall, it hurts and, from that pain, we may learn many lessons; therefore, souls descend into this world to experience concepts in matter—to feel, to experience. That's part of why we need each other. When someone says something to me that hurts me, it's experienced in the body, it's recorded, it affects who I am and shapes me as a person.

I come from an angry home. My dad would yell at every little thing, and I never knew if he was angry and yelling at me, at himself, or at someone else. When I became a mother, I too was an angry and screaming mother. My threshold for self-regulation was nil, and I could transform from complete serenity to screaming hysterically in seconds. I hated every minute of it. This led me to a process with myself. I had to learn to manage my anger, understand what was behind it, handle it, and even heal it.

The process I went through, facing the wounds I inherited from my father and my desire to be a different kind of parent than he was, transformed me into a therapist who helps angry people. It is thanks to my father's and my own anger that I am able to help people deal with their anger. As a soul, I chose an angry father, and even chose that he would scar me emotionally, so that I could grow from the experience and help others. My soul contract with my father contains many soul lessons, both his and mine. Part of the contract was the possibility of becoming a therapist. I became a therapist thanks to what I went through with my father. Thanks to my parents and my childhood, thousands of children in Israel experience better parenting. My father was also the writer in my family. I'm sure I chose him for that reason, too. While writing this book, my father died of cancer. This book is dedicated to him.

My soul contract with my father impacted me, and it also impacts you, dear reader. But that's my story. For someone else, the story could be different. We are four siblings in my family— all from the same home—and each dealt in their own way with my father and his screams. The contract could be overcoming impulsivity, building self-confidence, becoming an authority that will change the world, and so on. There are many reasons we chose our lives and relationships, and they chose us. At the soul level, all our motivations are pure, aimed at healing, overcoming difficulty, fostering growth, and sparking evolution; they are always exacted out of love for one another.

Our Contracts Are Different and Varied

The contract I have with my father is independent of the contract I have with my mother, and each of them has their own contract with me. In fact, a contract between souls is not mutual. What I, as a soul, come to learn from one person is different from what that person comes to learn from me.

On one of my personal spiritual journeys, I saw my mother and myself. I saw the commitment she made to me before I came down to Earth. I could see that her commitment was a difficult one—she would close her heart to me, not connect with me and, thus, emotionally abandon me. She would do this to help me embark on a journey to connect with my feelings. On this path, I would be able to open up to emotional work. When I saw the soul connection between us, I understood the love that was there for me, and I understood my soul's need to be abandoned.

If I had been born to an embracing and loving mother, I would not have been able to embark on the journey that led me to who I am today. I would not have been able to develop Karmic Constellations. And I would not be able to write this book. This is great love and commitment on the soul level of my mother and yet such pain on an emotional level for both my mother and myself.

As I write these lines, my heart expands towards my mother and her sacrifice. She made a sacrifice in this world, not just on a soul level. We had a very turbulent and painful relationship.

Those with Whom We Have Contracts

We can look at the essence of soul contracts in several ways. For instance, they can be divided into three different types:

- **Class/Status contracts:** parent–child, teacher–student, employer–employee, and so on.
- **Fellowship contracts:** friendships, classmates, siblings, teammates.
- **Equality contracts:** romantic partners, business partners.

Each contract has the purpose of personal development or support. There are contracts for growth and empowerment, like our best friends, that can teach us self-acceptance or simply be there for us and understand us, no matter what we go through in life, or a good relationship, in which we uplift and support one other.

There are contracts for specific moments in time, such as teachers at school, or a teacher of a particular method. And there are contracts of longer duration such as parenting, siblings, and relationships.

We can have several contracts with one person. For example, I can have several distinct contracts with my husband pertaining to our relationship, sexuality, and the parenting of our children. Any issue we deal with in which we have a lesson to learn can become part of a contract with someone. The contracts we have with others are not the same as the contracts that others have with us. The contract I have with my mother is completely different from the one she has with me. As I wrote before, her contract with me—as I perceived it—was for her to close her heart. What is my contract with her? I don't know.

Why do we need these contracts? What are they good for? Why is it impossible to grow and develop in the world of souls? Why should pain be experienced? The contracts are designed to advance our soul's development. We do not evolve in a vacuum. Furthermore, contracts are meant to help us free ourselves from the karma that we carry. Contracts are designed to help us break free of our karma by bringing us experiences that help us learn.

As we have established, a soul in the world of souls cannot evolve; it needs the physical body and communication with others for its development. To this end, we bring partners along for the journey, souls from our family of souls that, like us, incarnate in bodies and impact us, as we do them. Before they descend into the body, souls choose the physical family into which they will be born as a physical entity, meaning that each and every one of you reading this knew in advance, as a soul, which family you were being born into. What's more, you planned it together with them. My father and I, my mother and I, my siblings and I—we all chose to come together to this family and learn from each other.

Why Should We Influence the Contracts We Signed?

One of the questions I am often asked is: If the contract of my soul is supposed to help me grow and develop, doesn't changing the contract harm the personal and soul processes?

Traditional conceptions of karma would say that the contract cannot be changed, but we are in a new age that looks at things differently and, therefore, we have new options available to us. Changing a contract can actually be a process of accelerating personal development rather than harming it. In the past, soul contracts accompanied us our whole lives, as life expectancy was much shorter. Today, during the course of one lifetime, we can work on several issues that concern us; as a result, we can also work on changing the contracts of the current incarnation. The goal of our lives, and the goal of our personal development, is to improve our lives. If we are unhappy, there is nothing that says we have to remain that way. Change does not mean upending one's life; rather, it is about improving it.

Influencing the soul contracts we signed can change a lot of things. It can change family relationships—suddenly, I'm happy with my children, and there's no tension between us. It can change patterns—I stay in the same workplace, but my behavior changes, and suddenly, I'm happy at work. It can change the familial power dynamics, creating equality between spouses and opening up new lines of communication. It can also lead to divorce, resignation, and other life situations. Changing the contract means first clearing the old energy that created the contract and then bringing new energy to the relationship.

Soul contracts are not supposed to bind us for a lifetime, especially if it's not good for us. Contracts between souls can be changed and released, even here in the physical world.

There are contracts that cannot be renounced, such as those between parents and children, which cannot be canceled or released but can certainly be changed. In one of the Karmic Constellations courses I taught, a student brought up a difficulty she had been experiencing with her eldest son. Her goal was to improve the relationship with him. The Constellation session led to a previous incarnation in which, apparently, she and her son were two men, blood brothers or soul brothers. They were soldiers at war trying to escape. They tried to escape together. She died, and he survived. In her previous life, her job was to look after him. There, in that incarnation, she failed. Here, he returned as her son. In her experience, life with him was indeed a battlefield.

A week after the session she reported that, when she was near her son, there was no longer the sense of a battlefield. All the same, there was still hypervigilance within her. Her body was alert and waiting for something to happen. As I write this, only two weeks have passed since the session, and the Constellation is taking its time to take full effect. Her body is used to being tense, but I believe it will relax when the experience of being on a battlefield is no longer present.

When Past Meets Present

Latifah's story gives us a fascinating glimpse into soul contracts that were forged in other incarnations and are reflected in the current incarnation. Through this story, you can see how changing and releasing an unfavorable contract from the past significantly affects the present.

Latifah and her husband Mohammed, both of Arab descent, married and built a home in the United States. She followed him to his home country, where they lived together for a few years until he fell in love with another woman, and they divorced. Since their divorce, he has tortured her. He distanced her from two of her children, denied her a work visa, and brought difficulty to every aspect of her life.

We placed the following representations:

- Me in This Incarnation
- My Soul
- Mohammed
- Mohammed's Soul

As a facilitator, I never know what will come up. What possible story from the past could cause a man to abuse his wife in the present. We placed a representative for the contract that Latifah's soul signed with Mohammed and saw that she had a very hard time with Mohammed's soul. What happened there? What is the source of this difficulty?

We placed a representation of the previous incarnation in which the contract was created. A sense of despair overtook me as a facilitator. I had thoughts like, "Why did I agree to this session," "What happens if I don't succeed," and "I wish we had a Constellation of Representatives." (A "constellation of representatives" is a process in which other people act as representations for the client. Family Constellations was originally created in group work, where group members served as representatives for the client. Even today, it is possible to perform representative constellations in workshops or pre-booked sessions.)

Usually when I have such a powerful experience within me, it serves as a sign that there is something in the field that is not being recognized. So I shared my feeling with Latifah, and we continued with the session. The emotions arising from Latifah's side were flat and shallow. From my experience, this indicated that something important was being ignored—in most cases, it is pain.

I decided to check. I asked her to place a representative of "Pain from a Previous Life that No One Acknowledges." When the representation of pain entered the field, Latifah's soul felt abused and Mohammed's soul felt deep pain. We brought representations of Latifah in that incarnation and Mohammed in that incarnation. The full picture was then revealed.

In the previous incarnation, Latifah and Mohammed were two sisters: Latifah was the elder sister and she abused her younger sister (Mohammed). One of the ideas of karma is that the soul wants to experience the full spectrum of emotions and experiences that exist in the body; as a soul—if Latifah's soul abused Mohammed in a certain incarnation, there will come an incarnation in which it seeks to experience the opposite.

It's not a matter of punishment or revenge; it's a matter of the fullness of experience. A full experience is one experienced in several ways. For example, if we take the subject of money, there are so many ways to experience money. You can be born rich, or you can be born poor and earn money and become rich, or you can be born rich and die poor; you can be born into the middle class, and so on. There are so many ways in which we can experience an attitude towards money. Similar to the Rubik's cube experience shared in Chapter 1, the soul needs to experience a certain subject from several aspects and perspectives.

Many times in abusive partnerships, the representations of a previous life reveal a similar story with a reversal of roles. When the client sees the big picture and the soul sees that it got what it asked for, it can be released.

The lesson in this case is learned, and there is no longer a need to experience the abuse.

I believe that when a person opens their eyes to a higher truth they can release stores of pain and heaviness from their life. In this respect, Karmic Constellations allows people to connect with the perspective of the soul and see what happened in their life (as a soul) that led them to their life as it is now. When this happens, people can change and step onto a new path in life.

Back to the session. Beyond acknowledging the great pain that existed in that incarnation between Latifah and Mohammed, I felt that there was nothing I could do. In Karmic Constellations, I do not create corrective experiences; there is no way of changing the reality that existed in the past during the course of the session. What was, was. At the same time, the very recognition of what was, the very recognition of the pain, and taking responsibility for this pain, is significant and ultimately creates change.

When we, in the present incarnation, recognize the pain of the characters from previous incarnations, whether it is our pain from the previous life or the pain of another soul, movement occurs in the system—movement that brings about change and may even bring healing.

Latifah acknowledged Mohammed's pain in the previous incarnation, took responsibility for it, and even said that she had paid the price in full. Something also changed in Mohammed's representation. The atmosphere in the room, which had previously been one of great despair and pain, took on a different facet. A sense of lightness was created in the room and in Latifah, both in her representation and within herself as a person.

I believe that once we have felt and learned what we set out to and found its source, we are capable of doing what Kryon says: "Drop karma, for it is no longer suitable for the magnificence of who you are."

When we acknowledge the pain, hardship, and our actions in previous lives, we can release the karma of the previous incarnation, the one that created the current incarnation and what has occurred in it. Latifah can release what was when she understands that her abusive husband originated from a contract signed in another time and space when she abused him and that she holds this memory and thus, has agreed to his abuse in this lifetime. We can release karma when we take responsibility for what occurred in a previous life and what is occurring today, thereby separating the past incarnation from that of today.

It is up to us to acknowledge what this means, understand what happened, then and now, and accept it. The events themselves cannot be corrected or changed; one can only change the energy surrounding them. In addition, revealing the events that happened in the past allows us and our soul a deeper understanding of what happened and grants us an understanding of how this affects our conduct in the present.

In various methodologies that work with reincarnations, such as Past Life Regression, therapists often create a corrective experience at the moment of trauma; healing of the previous incarnation is done by creating an alternative reality. I found that this didn't work for me. As a result, my work focuses on acknowledging what is, taking responsibility, and creating a separation between the realms of the previous incarnation and this one.

What does it mean to take responsibility?

When representations of the previous incarnation and of the soul take responsibility for what happened, seemingly admitting to the crime, and saying, "Yes, that's what I did," it releases a lot of energy from the field. It frees energy from the representation and from the other representatives in the field. It touches stored, experienced trauma and releases energies that were trapped there. This renewed energy makes it possible to make a distinction between then and now.

"Past Life Me" was abusive and took responsibility for it, but in my current incarnation, I am not abusive. Once we acknowledge what is and take responsibility for it we, who are represented in this incarnation, can stop being caught up in our soul history. We can move into new spaces where the past has no foothold. We can say goodbye to the representation of ourselves from past lives and to the trauma associated with that past, and thus truly start over. The separation can occur when the client recognizes what was and takes responsibility, or when a representation of any kind, including the soul, tells the client that what happened in the past does not belong to them; that they don't have to bear the load of what happened.

In Latifah's case, she did not abuse anyone in her current incarnation. It was a past life version of her. Therefore, once the truth was revealed, she no longer had to carry the feeling that she must understand what it's like to be on the other side of cruelty. This new understanding enabled her to return this energy to the soul and the previous incarnation and to produce new energies, or lessons for the soul, that do not contain the feeling of guilt.

In Karmic Constellations, when I work on the relationship between two people, it usually involves soul contracts and shared karma. Most often, only one person comes to a Karmic Constellations session, even if the subject at hand involves a couple. In this case, I always say that it is possible to work on and create change only in the contract of the person in the session and not in the contract of the person who did not show up. As a therapist, it is important for me to respect the space of someone who has not consented to treatment and is not present for the processes involving them and their soul. Working with soul contracts works primarily on the person present in the session.

Shared Karma

When I facilitate a Karmic Constellations soul contract session, there will usually be six representations at the beginning of the session. For each of the two relevant parties we bring: representations of the client and of the person with whom the client person wants to explore her soul contracts, and representations of the souls of each person and of the contracts each has with the other. Only after all six representations are placed in space, do we examine what is happening in the field and what the relationships are between all the representations, and only then do we address the previous incarnation of these souls and what happened there. It works wonderfully. Nonetheless, the process can be over-wrought and, at times, feel unnecessarily cumbersome.

On one occasion, when I was hosting a session about the relationship of a woman and another person, I had the idea to bring a representation of shared karma instead of the soul contract of each. Shared karma is the combination of all the encounters in our previous lives and those of the other person, and it affects our current relationship in this life. Unlike a soul contract session, which usually leads the client and myself to a specific incarnation and relates to a specific issue that happened to us with the other person, shared karma can create the conditions for everything related to my relationship and that of the other person to be reflected during the session in full. Both the good and the bad.

Shared karma is less about the contract we have signed with each other, and more about the accumulation of shared energies we carry and contain within ourselves.

Additionally, when dealing with soul contracts, I work solely with my client and with the contract they signed with the other person. I don't involve the contract that the other party signed with the client. Working with shared karma allows everything that is currently right for the client to be cleared from their system, regardless of what belongs to them and what belongs to the other person, who is not currently in session.

Sheila's Story

When Sheila found Karmic Constellations, she sought to examine her relationship with Byron. I asked her to bring a representation of her and Byron's shared karma, and four incarnations arose with four distinct life stories. The first incarnation was a sibling experience. Byron was the older brother, and he was kept busy taking care of his little sister, Sheila, a child with special needs.

The second incarnation that arose was the memory of an elderly couple towards the end of their lives, living together in harmony.

The third incarnation evoked the memory of a couple who were both lovers and colleagues in their workplace, but the man, Byron, cheated on his partner, Sheila. We witnessed in the session that, despite the betrayal, Sheila's previous incarnation wanted to remain in a relationship with Byron because she loved him and was willing to come to terms with the betrayal.

The fourth incarnation was the memory of the two as platonic friends, devoid of romantic connection, spending time together and enjoying life.

These four incarnations impact Sheila's current relationship with Byron. This is especially true of incarnations that contain vast emotions: the incarnation of betrayal which evoked pain and the incarnation of the siblings in which Byron took care of Sheila. These two emotional imprints, which Byron carries within him, albeit unconsciously, now influence and even dictate Sheila's relationship with him.

In the session itself we made space for the sensations that arose from the experience; we acknowledged the pain that existed and, most importantly, we recognized that the Sheila and Byron of today are not the Sheila and Byron that they were in previous lives. This gave Sheila a sense of well-being and allowed her to move on, to break out of the patterns of previous lives and create something new, which is what she wished for herself.

When we see the past, when we understand it, when we make room for the pain we have caused and the pain that has been caused to us, it is easier to let go. It's easier to heal and choose new paths.

Exercise
Working with Soul Contracts

Karmic Constellations is a therapeutic modality, and it's not possible to convey complete therapeutic processes in a book. That being said, short exercises can be done to produce small changes or expand the knowledge of your experience. The following exercise can help you understand and feel the energy of a contract you have with a particular person. It can be anyone: spouse, parent, child, boss, and so on. When the contract is felt, the subconscious comes into play, and movement within our inner experience is possible. This exercise helps summon resources and change the energy and frequency of a contract. This is a short, structured exercise, not a full session. It is designed to allow you to deeply understand and shift the energies that motivate you.

The exercise requires six representations. We'll start with placing four representations and add the two remaining ones later:

- Me in My Current Incarnation
- My Soul
- The Person with Whom I Want to Research my Contract
- Their Soul

Place the four representations in front of you in any way that feels right and appropriate to you. Look at the placement of the representatives—which representations did you bring? How are they laid out? Are they close to each other? Are they far away? If they have faces, who's looking at whom?

How do you feel about this positioning?

Are you comfortable with it? Are you uncomfortable with it? Do you sense anything or nothing?

Now lay your hand on each representative. Give yourself some time—between 30 seconds and a minute—and notice what comes up within you.

What sensations do you feel in your body?

Are they pleasant or unpleasant?

Go through all the representations, and allow space for feelings and sensations to arise from each and every one.

Add a representative for the soul contract you have with that person. Now go back to each of the first four representatives and note whether anything changed in your sensation?

Now you must enter into your soul contract and pay attention to the sensations that arise in you. Are the sensations pleasant or unpleasant?

If the sensations are pleasant, that's great! These are feelings we want to have in the system. If the feelings are unpleasant, bring a representative for something that will provide strength to this contract. This is something amorphous. You're not supposed to know what it is. It is simply a resource. It can also be called "contract resource." Now place your hands on each of the first four representations you brought. Has anything changed in their energy?

Place your hand on "The Contract." Has anything changed in its energy?

> Place your hand on "The Resource." What is the feeling there? Stay with the sensation a bit longer. Allow yourself to be filled by this resource (even if you don't know exactly what it is).
>
> Take your hands off the representatives.
>
> Look again at the positioning. Are the representations laid out in a way that feels right to you? If so, great. If not, move them so that you feel more comfortable with how they are placed. After you've moved them, look at them. What are your feelings and sensations now?

This process can be done more than once; it is not a therapeutic process. Even so, it brings resources to the system and allows our subconscious to experience change by working on the representations, sensations, and emotions that arise.

Message from The Group about Soul Contracts

As I mentioned in the preface, during the editing of this book, channeling communications came through from The Group. In most chapters, their messages were organically integrated into the body of the chapter.

The Group message on soul contracts stands on its own. It has a different perspective from anything I've written so far. It has a frequency that is distinctly different from that of the frequency of the rest of the chapter. I chose to present the message in its entirety, as an extension to this chapter, for conscious, cognitive, and emotional reasons. Their message touched me deeply and created profound perceptual changes within me regarding the love inherent in the agreements we make with each other as souls. I hope this message touches you in the same way.

⁓

Beloved ones, before you come to this land you make agreements with others. Agreements are not contracts. We don't know why you chose such a rigid word as "contracts" when, in fact, they are agreements. The word "agreement" contains the word "agree." You agree with one another, you seek to make changes in the essence of your soul to overcome obstacles and to grow, to imprint knowledge and to experience whatever will lead to the knowledge that will change your soul. You see, the soul is not static; it has characteristics, and it wants to learn. It reincarnates in order to, among other things, expand the body of knowledge it has and change its characteristics. Just as a child looks at their parents and tells themself that they want to grow up and be like them, and in order to be like them they adapt behaviors and ways of thinking, and these in turn become their qualities in adulthood—so too does the soul choose what it wants to be, where it aspires to go, and adapts the qualities of consciousness that change and shape it. But unlike a child who has parents, the soul needs you, dear human beings, to enable this transformation. All this growth only happens when the soul is in your body, and parenting, by this analogy, is the experiments and experiences.

Although these contracts are binding and confining, you don't actually "sign" them. As we believe in choice from the outset, it would be more accurate to call them agreements. You agree with each other without "signing" these agreements—you might call it a handshake or verbal consent. You agree to be there for each other in your own way, for you understand that in order to acquire the knowledge you aspire to, you must experiment, and your agreements are designed to facilitate you helping each other with that. Agreement, to agree, contains a lot of energy, it contains choice.

You agree—no one forces it upon you; no one requires you to do so. You agree and choose to embody qualities of bad people, good people, murderers and murdered, abandoned and abandoners, and why? Because it teaches you a lot on a soul level and, therefore, before you come down to Earth, you consent; you choose with whom to do what and why; you agree to be with them, and they agree to be with you.

Agreement is such a beautiful word, our loved ones. If only you would see its softness, its gentleness, the sacred geometry inherent in this word, and the space within you that says "I agree." If we look for a metaphor from your world, then the best expression of this would be a couple standing at the altar, gazing with love and tenderness and passion and excitement for each other, as they say "I do" to the course of a life together. Imagine a picture of love—a couple of true lovers taking marriage vows, promising to follow each other through fire and water, which is a metaphor for life, of course. So, too, before you go down to Earth, do you stand before a crowd of souls, with all the souls you have chosen and who have chosen you to descend. So too do you stand in a large crowd of people and all say, "I do," and you walk with those people through fire and water, here on this earth. This is not a contract, and there is no judge sentencing you; it is an agreement to walk the path together. And, like any trip, it has ups and downs, hills and valleys, stunning views and barren wastelands.

We urge you, dear ones, to listen to the voice of your heart. Agreement is a choice, not a binding contract, not a punishment. The path is a choice. You are not a chained captive, and there is no one behind you pushing and prodding you to follow one path or another. It's just you, dear ones—only you and your agreements. And it's okay not to be up to the task, to stop halfway up the mountain and rest and even choose to descend, even though the goal was the summit. It's okay. If only you could see how much you are loved, no matter what you choose, you'd be softer with yourself. These are not marriage vows—"until death do us part." And what is death anyway? Physical death. And what about the death of the soul while it is still in this body? We do not encourage the death of the soul while in the physical body at all. We encourage deep and devoted listening to the beating of the heart and the call of the soul, which you agreed to experience before you came to Earth, but once you are here, you are free to change the agreement.

We do not suggest nor encourage giving up quickly— no, the soul is here to cope. But we do not promote perseverance at all costs. We do not encourage losing who you are for the sake of others. On the contrary, the goal is to find yourself, develop, and grow and connect to your divine being out of the tribulations and pains you have agreed to experience. And if that isn't working for you, you are allowed to change course. It's your choice,

your agreement, and your right to say no. How much
we love the word "agreement." If only you could see its
richness of energy, the love it contains, and its sacred
geometry. Agree to life, agree to the choices you have
chosen, and when you resist something from the bottom
of your being, agree to follow a new and different path.
No one will punish you at the end of your life. There is no
referee at the gate and no obligation to die because of
agreements made before you arrived.

It's all the path, and the path will go on and on beyond
this incarnation. Say yes to life, and live it through to its
end. This is your only contract, and it is yours with yourself,
your soul's with itself, and your soul's with you.

— The Group

Chapter 5

UNDERSTANDING
SOUL LESSONS

I go into the Akashic records. The book of my life opens, and I wonder which relationship I ought to work on (I have a lot of relationships that demand my attention, and I'm wondering which one will come up today). The connection between me and my eldest son emerges. I'm surprised. I had a few more urgent (or acute) relationships on my mind.

The book presents me with an image. He is a small, abandoned baby. Yearning for love, I scoop him up thinking that raising him will supply me with the love I seek when, in fact, what I lack in my life is self-love.

I exit the records and return to the here and now. No child can supply me with self-love. No partner can, either. Only I can give myself self-love. I understand the lesson and the message.

I leave the clinic and go home. My son and I arrange to go wash the car. I decide to take advantage of the situation and tell him what I saw. A whole discourse develops about souls, reincarnation, parenting, the role of souls, and more. At the end of it he asks, "But Mom, if you learn the lesson, does that mean that in the next life I won't be born? What will happen to me?" I miss the mark with my answer because I don't really understand the question. On the surface, I've answered the question he asked—that he doesn't have to reincarnate as my child; he can reincarnate into anything next time. But the real question he's asking me is a question about love: Mom, if you learn to love yourself, then will you not need me anymore to learn how to love? And the answer I had to give was: When I learn to love myself, I can raise him without using him as a tool. I won't need him to teach me something he can't. When I learn to love myself, I will be able to see him as he is, effortlessly, and he will be able to love himself, too.

This conversation took place when my son was 18. He's old enough and an independent thinker, but we're all our parents' children, wanting our parents to see us in our three-dimensional fullness and to approve of our whole selves.

Each of us has their own lesson. Soul lessons are the soul's choice to learn something, and they are expressed in different ways in our lives. We choose to tackle a certain issue in our lives in order to grow and evolve. Unlike a soul contract, which is like a system of agreement between me and the other, a soul's lesson is entirely ours. We won't always conquer our soul lesson but, as souls, we always try.

At the time I was writing these lines, the business space (the building in which the editor of my book worked) burned down, and the question of soul lessons and their essence was reinforced in our discourse. Things happen to us in life and will always do so. Some are good, and others are bad. The soul lessons deal with how we handle ourselves—how we address or avoid what has happened to us and what we learned along the way. Like my father's cancer—how I coped with it, with my father's treatment, what I learned from it, and what I avoided dealing with.

There will always be a gap between the soul's choice and how we actually live our lives. No one deliberately and consciously chooses to be poor or to have a malignant or incurable disease. But the soul does choose. We live out the choices of the soul and, through the body, we experience these choices and must contend with them.

Soul lessons usually incorporate various topics, such as career, money, self-image, self-acceptance, love, and so forth, rather than relationships. Of course, any contract with another person can contain a soul lesson. In Karmic Constellations, I look for the the trauma or the issue that created the soul lesson, and there I seek to release the painful energy that affects the present incarnation.

The soul contract we sign with another soul was created to help and support the soul lessons we have chosen to undergo here in this lifetime. My son came to teach me, and I came to teach him. My lesson is to learn self-love—love that does not depend on the other person. When I learn this, I will develop as a soul and then, in the next life, I may no longer deal with lessons in self-love; and my son, who reincarnates with me (if he reincarnates with me) may not come as a child to a mother struggling with her motherhood, but as a friend, brother, or something else. Maybe he will come again as my child and this time we will choose to learn things that have nothing to do with love or self-worth. Between us there are so many lessons that parenting teaches us as human beings and souls, and it is impossible to learn everything in one incarnation.

What Are Soul Lessons?

When The Group gave me an explanation of what soul lessons are, I felt that it was describing the subject so beautifully that

I left the message intact, without interpreting or expanding. Here's what The Group had to say about soul lessons:

It's like the game of hopscotch. It's a social game, a competitive game, a fun game. When you play hopscotch, you have to go from 1 to 2 and then to 3, and sometimes you can't switch to 3, because 3 is built a little differently; usually the square of 3 is on the side and, if you fall and your foot steps out of bounds, you have to go back and do everything all over again.

You do not have to go back to the beginning with soul lessons. But it's okay to linger at 3 a little longer, and it's also okay to try and go back to 3 again and again and again. There is nothing sizing you up, no judgment. They want to get to 10 in hopscotch. What fun it is to get to 10. But it's also okay not to get to 10. It's the way that matters, the game, not the result or the win. Am I enjoying the path? How many times do I only manage to reach number 3 or number 4? Will I be able to get to 6, which is farther on the board? After all, you can't jump straight to number 6. To get to 6, you have to go through all the stages, all the numbers in front of it. To get to the possibility of reaching number 6, you may have to play more than once.

Few are those who reach 10 in ten tries. Most people fall at some point along the way, get stuck at some point, and fail to throw the stone to the number they intended. They may have thrown at 3 but reached 4, but you can't jump to 4 without going to 3 first. The hopscotch game can be likened to soul lessons. Soul development is the game.

The joy and the frustration of children—the joy when they succeed, the frustration when they fail—and the other children who stand around and cheer, not all but some of them, there is brotherhood here, there is play, there is innocence, there is naivety and, yes, there is a desire to cross the finish line.

In hopscotch, like in soul lessons, we want to get to the finish line, we want to see things as they are, we want to finish the subject and, at the same time, we may have to go back and practice numbers 3 and 6 over and over again, and we can't get to six without going through 1, 2, 3, 4, 5.

Soul lessons are measured by how you, dear people, learn, not with success or failure. Sometimes progress will be only one millimeter, but that millimeter is a lot, because you didn't have it before. Sometimes progress will be ten steps, and there is no one step similar to another, and no lesson similar to another, so you may advance ten steps in your lesson with money but, with your body image, only a millimeter. No one stands at the end and checks on you.

The soul lessons are yours, they are your desire to overcome and learn and experience more, and it's okay if you don't succeed. There's no one standing at the gate telling you, "Come on!" We applaud when you succeed and we're with you, holding you through your pain, when you don't, and yet, that's what the next incarnation is for. To this end, the dice or stones can roll again, each time in a different direction, in a different way, and each time you learn new things. Each body will give you a different experience. Jumping in hopscotch when you're three is very different from doing it when you're seven; different as a girl, as a boy; different when the crowd is girls cheering you on or boys cheering you on. No game of hopscotch is like another. Not one. Even if the drawing of the hopscotch board is always the same, even if you still use chalk.

The same goes for incarnations; no two incarnation are alike. Each time more knowledge and more learning accumulates, and in the end comes the place of peace, or there comes a place where the soul chooses not to learn or chooses to go back and learn things it has forgotten; this is also an option. There are no end goals. Do you know people who ask whether this is their last incarnation? It's up to the soul to decide and, when it ascends, it's all a game. Everything is an experience—even the worst of experiences is an experience. It's a soul choice.

— The Group

What Does the Soul Come Here to Learn?

The soul is an extension of the Creator—the Source. It is the Creator and the Source and is, therefore, eternal. The soul's connection with the body is what allows it to learn about itself, and it is what supplies its challenges, obstacles, successes, and experiences—some successful and others not.

Learning is not a one-time thing. In school we learn that 1+1=2 and, as far as we're concerned, we've learned the lesson and there's no need to delve deeper into it. But the way the soul learns is process and evolution. Many times the learning develops over our entire life and other times it develops over several incarnations. And no, we don't have to succeed in our learning. And that's okay. The soul, unlike us, has time. It is in no hurry to get anywhere.

As part of our learning, there are soul lessons that we must go through. Some are small and others large. Each of us has lessons that the soul chooses. The choice of soul lessons, as I see it, depends on two factors: first, choosing soul lessons related to past experience—things that the soul has already experienced and wants to bring healing to or strengthen; and second, choosing soul lessons related to new things the soul wants to learn.

Lessons related to past experience

Our past is full of trials, and these can be milestones in our learning if only we allow them to be. When preparing to reincarnate, the soul chooses which qualities it wishes to develop or issues it wishes to overcome. The soul examines which skills it has developed in previous lives that it wants to continue developing in the current incarnation. A skill can be anything—from developing the tools to become a therapist, artist, writer, actress, and more, to more general qualities such as humility and modesty.

In one of the Constellation Labs, when I was investigating the choices of the soul regarding the family system—which soul would reach which sibling or, for example, why my soul chose to be the first to reach my parents—I also investigated the meaning of choosing the order of arrival into the world. Helena, one of the participants, brought her family set-up: she is the oldest, her sister is the middle child, and her brother is the youngest. When we tested the order from a soul standpoint, what came up in the lab was that the middle sister's soul wanted to practice "invisibility": that is, to be the one who was not seen. How is this possible?

In the culture from which Helena comes, the firstborn boy or girl is important in terms of the roles of responsibility they require. In addition to this, there is a yearning for sons. As soon as the first son is born, no matter what his position among the siblings, he is considered the firstborn. As Helena was the first daughter born into this family, she was given the role of being responsible and a stand-in for the mother. The son, born third, assumed the role of the "man," continuing the dynasty of the family. The middle child does not have a significant role for parents. A child in this role often "disappears" and is seemingly less significant. In this way, the soul can develop the skill of "invisibility."

At first glance, being invisible doesn't seem like a skill we would want to acquire, and I believe that Helena's sister does not necessarily have it easy in life, but for the soul it means something, and there is a reason why she chose to practice this skill (we did not examine the reason in the lab—that was not the purpose of the lab).

In addition to developing new skills, the soul often chooses lessons to help overcome difficulties it has experienced in previous lives, such as arrogance, stinginess, temperament, anxiety, fear and more. Most of what we must overcome depends on traumas from past lives.

Many therapists (both men and women) were once healers and spiritual disciples in ancient traditions. We can see that the history of most of these healers is bloody. Sometimes they experienced a real witch hunt, but sometimes it was enough that they were healers who lived in a tribe and they were unable to save the daughter of the tribal chief, which doomed them to death. This soul history of healers can haunt these souls and, when they reincarnate, despite their soul's yearning, they experience an inner fear of doing what their soul desires.

At the same time, they are here as healing souls, practicing some form of medicine, and the healers they have incarnated within feel that something is blocking them from advancing and acquiring more knowledge, or from sharing their gifts to more and more people. Just as these souls have a fear of death because of their occupation, we too contain within us memories related to fear of death (or other fears) that prevent us from realizing ourselves fully in this incarnation. We may want to achieve something, to engage in something, and even feel a strong calling for that thing, but we may find that we repeatedly experience difficulties, fail to do the thing, fail to achieve it, and we do not understand why.

For many years, every attempt I made to form a parental support group robbed me of a lot of energy. No matter how much I aimed at achieving this goal, or how deeply I wanted to do so, the groups either didn't open or opened with a small number of registrants. It made no difference that I'm a certified group facilitator, that I love teaching, that I was actually born to teach (just not in a standard school), and that I very much enjoy facilitating groups. Nothing happened.

I experienced great frustration.

I know from this incarnation what the difficulty with group facilitation stems from, and I worked on it for many years—still, nothing changed. Then came the Karmic Constellations and the ability to open up to prior, even ancient, information. I stand in for the representation of myself in a previous life, which has to do with my difficulty with groups, and I "remember" hundreds of years back. I am the head of a village. We have two options: surrender to our occupiers or die battling them. The village I lead makes a decision to die fighting. We don't want to be conquered, and we're willing to die for it. When the occupiers reach our village, we go to war against them, and we die. An entire village with all its men, women, and children die in the war. I carry with me great pain—the pain of responsibility. I never want to bear that responsibility again. I am at peace with my decision as the head of the village, but not at peace with the massive loss of life that took place, for which I, in part, am responsible.

I sit for several long minutes in the embodiment of this representation, experiencing the war and the pain first-hand. Being the head of a village is indeed a great responsibility. So is being a group facilitator, despite the many differences between the two. No group I lead will be asked to choose between life and death. I facilitate personal development and learning—not the government of villages. The level of responsibility is totally different, as is the manner of implementation. A village is not a group that comes together for a discrete period of time to undergo a process and then return home.

I make a distinction between that incarnation and this one. I'm not her, and she's not me. I let go of the trauma and absorb the teachings. She was the head of a village. She must have a lot of good things to teach me that I can bring into my life today. When I let go of the trauma, I can enhance the learning and make more progress in my life.

This session did release some sort of block within me regarding group facilitation. While I didn't start a parental support group, life led me to let go of my work with parents and focus on my work on karma and the karmic space, and I found it much easier to start groups.

So what did my soul come to learn from these events? Perhaps my soul wanted to explore different types of responsibilities; perhaps it was about different modalities of leadership. My challenge in facilitating groups is also related to this incarnation, to the world in which I grew up—within an oppressive group, in a kibbutz for 15 years. My challenge was to overcome the childhood traumas that I, as a soul, chose to experience, to let go of past lives, and to bring my knowledge to as many groups as possible.

Lessons related to new things
the soul wants to learn

As I previously mentioned, many soul lessons are related to our past experiences. That being said, the soul may want to learn new things that it has never been exposed to or interested in before. For example, a soul can, after reincarnating in the same place or gender multiple times, choose to change gender or place. If they have developed their intellectual or spiritual skills in their travels through various incarnations, they may want to develop athletic abilities and learn new facets of experience that they have not been exposed to before.

This is what happened with Selena who came to me to explore the subject of femininity in her life. Selena is a woman of Indian descent, married, without children, who lived in France and worked in the male-dominated world of tech. She said that being a woman was difficult because she felt more connected to the masculine; she thrived on competition, connected to the male mentality, and her career was more important to her than marriage and the idea of motherhood. At the same time, she did not feel that she belonged to the male environment she was in, because she was a woman and she longed to feel good in her body, to feel good about her womanhood, to connect with her feminine side, and to embody softer characteristics in her personality and life.

We stood in front of the Council between Incarnations (a space where the soul meets higher souls that support its journey, reflects on the incarnation just completed, and decides what to learn in the next life) and asked the council what it was about femininity that Selena needed to learn. We found out that, for many years, Selena was a man and therefore, feminine behavior is still difficult for her, but she is here to learn and develop more and more feminine qualities. She has come to Earth in this life to develop her feminine energy, and her therapeutic side. In this case, Selena's soul chose to change gender in order to learn feminine behavior and develop through it. Selena's difficulty with her sense of femininity stemmed from a multi-incarnation soul experience of being a man rather than a woman.

Disability, Illness, and Physical Limitation

As I see it, learning disabilities, physical or mental illnesses, and physical limitations (as well as any other naturally occurring disorders) are not lessons, but rather, expressions or embodiments of the way we have chosen to learn. Many times, a disease holds within it memories of the past. It may arise from traumas that have happened to us and been repressed or not fully dealt with. The books of alternative medicine, as well as my clinic, are full of people who recovered once the memories surfaced and healing work was initiated. However, a certain illness or disability may also be the way a soul chose to live (and yes, die) in this world.

As human beings, the perception that the soul has chosen a life of illness is difficult for us, since illness is difficult. At the same time, a soul can learn a lot from experiencing paralysis, degeneration, cancer, and more. When we look at illness as a punishment, we are overlooking the great opportunity hidden within it to grow and develop. I don't dismiss the difficulty. It's there.

When I wrote these words, I had been accompanying my father through his three-year battle with cancer, which came and went. I was his primary caregiver. It was difficult. There were moments when I felt like I'd been punished for something. There were moments when I wished it would all be over so it would be easier for me. And there were moments when I wanted to collapse.

At the same time, I kept asking myself, What can I learn? What can I learn about my relationship with my father? What can I learn about my relationship with my mother? (My parents were divorced, *and* they had a good relationship.) What can I learn about my relationship with my siblings? What can I learn about my conduct through all of this?

These questions teach me a lot. They flood me with childhood memories, as well as remembrances of past lives, and they take me on a journey of unraveling unhealthy relationships from past lives and releasing previous roles, perceptions, and behaviors from those incarnations. The difficulties we encounter in our lives are an invitation and an opportunity for consciousness and soul growth.

In January 2023, my father passed away from cancer. The night before his burial, he came to me through a channeled message and shared with me a truth about himself and his life. The message, I must admit, surprised me a lot. I feel that this knowledge, despite being personal, is intended for everyone. And therefore I choose to share it here:

> The world is much more complex than good and evil.
> People experience pain.
> People come to this world to experience pain.
> I came to this world to experience pain.
> It was my choice.

There was agreement between Matthew and myself [Matthew was my father's identical twin brother. Matthew died at the age of one and a half from a fever]. I did something very bad to him in another life, and I came here to experience the wound I inflicted. I have something to fix. I have something to improve upon as a soul, and the pain shapes and refines the soul. I have more lessons to learn. The road is not over. The choice of pain and suffering is not over. For too many years I have incarnated on the bad side.

I came to learn what love is. It's a hard lesson to learn. The feeling of unworthiness is a feeling that stems from the soul's desire to change, grow, and develop. The traumas are carefully chosen. Matthew was carefully chosen.

Earth is a deceptive mirror that does not reflect the world of souls.

The good and the bad, the joy and pain, the gentleness and the rudeness are reflections that do not necessarily properly express the soul.

I chose this body and this family to refine myself. It was my way of experiencing humility. There is no good without bad.

When a soul, which in its past incarnated on the surface of this sphere and did mostly evil deeds, was on the side of arrogance, cunning, haughtiness, illegal deeds, and so on, decides to change and bring goodness and tenderness and gentleness into its life, it's a process.

It doesn't all happen at once. There are many energies that need to change.

There are many frequencies that need to be balanced.

The journey of growth and evolution cannot be easy.

It's not easy.

The soul arrives at a carefully chosen body and life experiences. It knows what's in the records. It knows what energy will be available to it. The energy availability in the records is predetermined. This is what the soul sets out to learn.

Of course, there are other energies and, on the journey to personal development, they open up and are revealed, but for starters—along the way, there are "unpleasant" energies.

And I chose this life to refine myself. Spiritually and mentally, not intellectually. I needed a body and a detached life experience. I needed the pain to develop and grow.

To refine.

You refuse to call it reward and punishment, but it is.

Or so I feel.

Pain has meaning. It comes to atone for the pain a person has caused others and also to teach them this side of things. It teaches them what it's like to be the victim. I hurt Matthew several incarnations ago, a fatal injury that left him helpless for many years. He came to teach me that.

There was no brotherhood in my soul and no soul twin. This was so in order to learn a hard lesson about loss and helplessness. It came to scar me in such a way that I would no longer have the arrogance and evil I had in previous lives.

Souls choose a life of suffering in order to be refined. The blows a person experiences in their life are also meant to refine them, their soul. And yes, they're also related to past lives.

About a month after his passing, my guidance told me more about my father's and my learning, especially in the context of caring for him while he was suffering from cancer:

In previous lives, where my father was a cold-hearted man, and even in a lifetime where he and I had a chance encounter that probably led to my death, he stood by. He never offered help to those he hurt. Now, in this incarnation, he experienced what it was like not to stand idly by, but quite the opposite since, ostensibly, I had every reason not to support my father and leave him to deal with his cancer on his own. Based on the way he raised me, I could find reasons within myself not to take care of him and let him cope alone and maybe even die alone.

But I refused to let my and my father's history dictate my relationship with him. It's against my values. Today, I also understand that it would be against my soul's contract with my father, the one related to cancer. Cancer was the way my father experienced unconditional giving, and standing by him all these years was mine, my little sister's, and his friends'. This is a lesson his soul will take with it for the rest of the way. I have no doubt about it.

Is It Possible to Replace or End Soul Lessons?

This is a very common question in the world of soul therapy. Let me begin by saying that, in my opinion, there is no one definite answer. It depends on the session, on the lesson and, just as importantly, on who is willing to release or be released. There are processes I facilitate where the lesson itself "tells" me that it's over and that the client no longer needs this lesson. And that's okay. We are here to complete lessons, to heal, to overcome obstacles and challenges, and to develop and grow.

So, yes, there are lessons that the soul has finished having to hold onto. Alternatively, there are cases in which the human will, which is not always the same as the soul's divine will, cannot decide, since it is not synchronized with the lesson. Yes, there are difficult lessons that we have chosen for ourselves. Why? For many reasons, not all of which are revealed to us as human beings. Even if we turn to mediums or various alternative treatments, there will still be motives that are hidden from us so that we can follow our own path.

Can we change lessons or end them? I think that if the lesson is over, it changes on its own. It helps if we bring awareness to the space. This allows it to change faster. But it depends on the soul, not the person.

Chapter 6
RESTORING SOUL FRAGMENTS

At its core, our soul is complete and full. It is one, if it can be defined in such a linear way. Imagine a battery, the one with the Energizer bunny that never depletes. We'd all wish to be that indomitable bunny, right? Well, the truth is, by and large as souls, we are like that. When we were created, we were like a fully charged battery.

I first heard the term "soul fragments" about 15 years ago, when a teacher from the Curanderismo tradition arrived in Israel and I went to her to learn how to recall soul fragments. Working in this method was cumbersome. You needed mattresses, two caregivers, and a client devoted to the process. According to that teacher, as a client, I did not devote myself to the process, although I swear I tried and had every sincere intention of doing so.

After the disappointing experience, and following the realization that restoring soul fragments required complex logistics, I released the desire to do this type of work and continued my usual energetic work, without recalling soul fragments.

As I continued to treat more and more people through energetic work, I noticed that soul fragments began to appear in the treatments I did—soul fragments from previous lives frozen in time. In an energetic process, according to what my intuition had guided me and suited the moment, I helped my clients regain their soul fragments. It didn't happen often but when it did, the client felt a change within—like another piece of the puzzle of their identity had been put in place.

What Are Soul Fragments?

Often when a very big trauma occurs in our lives, part of our soul splits from us. It is a kind of defense mechanism of the mind and soul designed to keep us safe so that we do not experience pain; that is, the body remains present, but the psyche/soul does not—it detaches from the body. Disengagement helps us cope with overwhelming fear and terror and keeps us numb to the event that took place in our lives. All this happens out of a need to protect and preserve the soul/psyche.

In fact, trauma cuts off parts of our soul. These parts then "disappear" from the whole and affect our progress and conduct in the world. Many times what happens is that our battery starts to reduce its capacity for replenishment. The disconnections that come from trauma rob us of a lot of energy, which then affects the rest of our conduct in the world. Additionally, the part of the soul that has been disconnected from us remains frozen in time; it does not grow up or develop alongside us.

In one of the workshops I facilitated a participant brought in a topic that was important to her. We did not deal directly with the issue of soul fragments, but the person who represented the participant said that everything was dark and that she was alone and felt like a little girl. When I asked the participant if the story was familiar to her, or if it had resonated with her, she said that at the age of four her father was angry with her and, as punishment, locked her in the shower in the dark for what felt like an eternity. After the story came up I realized that I was facing a sliver of her soul that remained frozen during that experience. Although the participant was over forty, this part of her soul remained four years old and, in fact, never left that dark shower. It stayed there. It did not go through the journey of growth and development that she and her soul had been through.

In another case, during an energy work session with the client, a fragment of soul that had remained in a previous life came to the client's field and wanted to reconnect with the soul. It was a soldier in the British Army who died in battle. This part of the soul remained a soldier in the British Army, on the battlefield, just before his death. That fragment did not undergo the return to the world of souls and did not become the woman who lay on the couch. Whether it disconnected from us in this incarnation or in another, these parts of our souls remain missing.

If we return for a moment to the metaphor of the battery, then the soul is an eternal battery. It is always full and allows full and fault-free usage. But if there are issues with the battery or how fast the battery runs out, it can be harder or sometimes impossible to use the device. Each such disengagement of fragments diminishes our strength; that is, reduces our ability to create, to be creative, to cope with life, and to build our mental and physical stamina.

It is important to note that soul fragments can arise from various events. They can be caused by great trauma (such as a murder, rape, car accident, war, and more), and they can be created from trivial events (moments when we held our breath in panic or anxiety and something, a particle, disconnected from us). In the Hebrew language, the words "soul" and "breath" share the same root—breathing. The soul and the breath are connected, and when there is a break in the breath it affects the soul.

When Daan van Kampenhout, a facilitator and teacher of Shamanic Constellations, gave a workshop in Israel he shared with us how he works with soul fragments through the constellation. It was the first time I had heard it could be done. I liked the idea and decided to experiment with soul fragments at The Systemic Lab. I discovered that it was possible for this process to be carried out in Karmic Constellations, and that fragments of the soul could be reconnected, thus making the soul fuller and allowing broader healing for the subject the client brought in.

How Are Soul Fragments Related to Changing Karma?

It's easier to make changes when we're at our best, feeling healthy and resilient. As we regain more and more parts of ourselves, from this or previous lives, our coping ability increases and life changes can be made more easily.

Restoring soul fragments mainly helps our mental resilience. It can be likened to life with full belly-breathing versus life with shallow breath. When we breathe fully, we are healthier and experience more of life. When we live with shallow breath, even a slight effort will cause us to stop and regulate our breathing.

I have often found in Karmic Constellation sessions that when a client comes in with a certain stagnation in their life it is not necessarily caused by trauma. In other words, healing the trauma will not be the thing that will lead the client to change, but rather, the work with the soul-split created by the trauma. When the soul retrieves the fragment and the parts become whole, the ability to process the trauma increases. Sometimes the return of the fragment embodies the healing of the trauma. When this happens, the stagnation is usually released.

When we encounter a sliver of soul, our goal as facilitators is to unite it with the soul, so that the soul will be more complete, since it is a part of it. Think of a part of a finger that has been cut off from a person: They can live without it, but they will have to learn how. On the other hand, if we manage to connect the missing part, when the incision heals and the finger becomes intact again, it will be easier for the person to function.

Challenges to Recovering Soul Fragments

Experience has taught me that in a constellation it is not necessarily easy to unite soul fragments with the soul. There's a lot of mistrust there. Often the fragment that remains frozen in time feels abandoned or forgotten. Although it longs to return to the soul from which it was detached, it struggles with feelings of anger and disbelief. It still carries the physical consciousness of whoever they disconnected from.

And the soul too has changed. It has undergone processes. Sometimes the divide between the soul and its part makes it difficult for the soul to accept the part that was frozen in time.

What can be done? I searched for ways to connect the fragment and the soul. It was clear to me that this was a process in which one had to work on the deeper layers of the soul's energy and not as much on a conscious level. I searched for a process that would work entirely on the unconscious.

Ever since I began my work in energy healing, I have been practicing channeled singing. I call it "channeled singing" because these are words and sounds that come out of me often from an uncontrollable impulse, and I don't understand what I'm singing or saying. I don't come from a musical background; on the contrary, most of my life can be defined as being "off key." Therefore, channeled singing is something I do when the urge arises and not as an integral part of my treatments. Today, there are many studies that show that music has a healing effect. For example, according to Chinese medicine, we know that every organ in the body has a sound, as does every chakra.

In one of the Karmic Constellations sessions I hosted, there were two representations, a soul and a fragment of that soul, and they refused to come near one another. Nothing moved in the session. I realized that I needed something different from the techniques I usually use, and I started singing. I didn't know if it would work or not, and I didn't know how the fragment and soul would react. When I finished singing and asked them how they felt, they reported feeling less constricted and subsequently moved closer to each other.

Since then, when I meet soul fragments in the clinic and want to create a connection between them and the soul, I use the channeled singing. The words, sounds, and voices that emerge create movement in the field. My students, who don't come from the world of channeled singing, play energy music. Any music that seems right to you at the moment will do the trick. The vibrations of music affect the space and produce a change in the vibration of the representatives. In my experience, it softens the pain each side feels and helps them release their rigidity and mistrust. The music softens and thus allows the two to get closer. It's not always enough, but it brings them closer.

When a soul fragment is returned to the body, it takes time for the body and energy to adjust. If I'm a 50-year-old woman now, my body behaves accordingly—it's not the body of a four-year-old girl, nor does it contain the energy of a four-year-old. It follows that I will need time to get used to new energy, frequency, and experience. The same applies if I'm a woman and the fragment is a male British soldier. I have to adapt to the frequency of a man and a soldier, as well as the mannerisms of a British person (which are very different from those of an Israeli). The synchronization between the energies takes time beyond the boundaries of the therapeutic session.

At such moments, I give instructions to clients for how to continue the process in their daily lives until the fragment is completely integrated with the soul. When the process ends, we feel more whole, have more inner strength, and are fortified by our inner light.

Talia's Story

Talia's story gives an example of a soul fragment and its process of integration with the soul. The theme Talia brought to the space was a feeling she carried within her that she described as a feeling of darkness that had accompanied her for her entire life. We placed representatives:

- Me in the Current Incarnation
- My Soul
- Darkness

The first thing Talia saw when she stood in for her own representation was a girl in a well. She was there because she was thrown in. When a representation of someone who is not "me" comes up, while standing in for the representation of "me" as a facilitator, I immediately know that we are dealing with a previous incarnation and want to bring a representative for that incarnation and hear what their story is.

We placed a representative for the girl in the well. The field revealed that she was kidnapped from her parents by someone and put in the well. The darkness turned into a multitude of faces and negative emotions. I asked her to bring representations of those to whom the darkness belonged. A group of people arrived.

The session went on, the representations expressed feelings and sensations, but there was no movement—no representative moved anywhere. I thought about the girl alone in the well, kidnapped from her parents, lonely and scared. I decided to see if there was a soul fragment left in the well. Talia placed a representative of the soul fragment that remained in the well. Suddenly, things moved. The representatives expressed many feelings and emotions like before, but this time they also moved. The stalemate from the field was released. Engaging the representation of the soul fragment was an acknowledgment of what was missing, after which the session could go on towards healing.

My goal in Talia's session was to unite the soul fragment, which had been frozen in age and in another incarnation, with Talia's soul as it was in the here and now of 2022.

The channeled singing helped dissolve much of the fear and pain, but there was still more left. I felt that more acknowledgment was needed for the child's fear and pain contained in the fragment, and I instructed the fragment to express this to the soul. As the fragment shared with the soul the fears and pains it held within, Talia understood that it was her light. She felt that the soul and the fragments were like shining stars in the sky, and eventually she was able to recognize that she was the light and allow the fragment to assimilate into the soul.

Exercise
Restore Soul Fragments

I perform this exercise whenever I feel tired and have no strength. It can be done on a daily basis.

Close your eyes, take a few deep breaths and concentrate inside. Feel your feet on the ground/floor or, if lying down, feel your back supported by the bed.

Feel your body fully.

Let go of all thoughts, and relax the body.

Say to yourself: "I recall to me all parts of my soul from all over the universe and existence."

Now just imagine them coming to you and filling you up. There is no one right place where they are supposed to go. They can enter the body from anywhere.

Pay attention to the sensations that arise in you. You may have a range of feelings. Just let the sensations be.

Take a few deep breaths to help the fragments enter and integrate.

Say to the fragments: "Thank you for returning to me, to my body, and to my soul."

Pay attention to the sensations in the body. Take a few more deep breaths, and open your eyes.

The Group and Soul Fragments

The channeling I received from The Group about soul fragments surprised me. On the surface, it negates my work. But the truth is that it doesn't do that at all; it just offers another lens. So I decided to put it here at the end of the chapter. I invite you to accept all the perspectives in this chapter and allow them to expand your consciousness.

"Soul fragment" is a very amusing definition for the way you perceive the soul; seeing the soul as an entity that can separate parts of itself. And we want to tell you, contrary to what is written here in this book, and contrary to popular belief for many years, there really is no such thing as "soul fragments." Yes, there are memories that remain frozen in time, yes there are energies that remain, but the soul as a soul is always whole, inseparable from itself.

Saying "soul fragments" is a bit like cutting the source into pieces. The source is always intact, and so is the soul. It knows how to contain the worst pain that exists on Earth. The body does not; the human structure does not. Therefore, the loss of these parts has been called "soul fragmentation" over the years. And that's okay. We're okay with that part, for your being needs this knowledge, this space. The return of soul fragments enables the growth of consciousness, acceptance of the past, and return of forgotten parts. It's a bit like shadow work. Fragments are shadows. They are shadows that accompany you, even through the transition from incarnation to incarnation, because the soul, the soul seeks to expand, seeks to be uniform, in congruence, with everything it has ever gone through and everything it will ever go through, and these fractures, the separation of human being, the separation that is required for being human, prevent the mind and the soul from expanding.

We have come to tell you that there really is no such thing as soul fragments. There are fragments of consciousness. We know that soul fragment work is deep shamanic work, and we are not here to undo centuries of work so important and significant to human mental health because, when the mind splits, it is like a soul fragment. When the human mind cuts off a memory and there is fragmentation in a person's being, it is like a fragment of a soul.

In Hebrew there is a difference between soul and psyche. If we take the Hebrew terms, we will say that these are fragments of a person's psyche and not fragments of their soul. [Psyche is not accurate; there is no proper English translation for the Hebrew term.] And the body remembers everything, even the fragments that were forgotten by the soul. The body remembers, even though the body is perishable and the soul moves on to other incarnations. The new body remembers the fragments of the psyche. They are deeply hidden in the structure of DNA. Imagine spiritual-soul epigenetics, not intergenerational transmission. That's where the fragments of your soul are, in spiritual-soul epigenetics. And you live with these splits constantly. And they yearn deeply to return. Your soul yearns to return the lost parts and feels like a lost child, because you lost something significant when the split happened. We rejoice in this work, and we understand why it is easier to call it "soul fragments" as Yael and shamanic tribes do. For these are absolutely parts of you that have been lost. And as you complete, receive, and return these parts to yourself, your being becomes more complete. Your consciousness becomes more complete, and you can contain more which, in turn, heals the soul—and when the soul is complete, the soul is well.

Anything you do to heal the soul and bring back more and more parts of itself, parts lost over time, over generations, over reincarnations, helps. The more work you put into restoring those parts, the more the soul can grow—because its capacity, its ability to contain, will increase. The soul that descends to this Earth does not stand on its own; it is connected to the body, to the records, to the biological memories of consciousness of all time, and these memories also contain what has been lost, what has not been given its place for one reason or another. And every return, each connection, allows the soul to evolve and expands the consciousness. You are more full of your own being. This is the return of fragments at its best. We, The Group, encourage you to continue your significant and important healing work.

— The Group

Chapter 7

VOWS, CURSES, AND KARMA

In Judaism, we celebrate the holy day of Yom Kippur, which is the time to release vows, seek atonement, and ask for forgiveness. I am writing these words on this holy day. I take advantage of the auspicious time to connect to the frequency of this day and, as I write, I hold within myself the knowledge that it is okay to undo vows and curses at any time, no matter what culture and religion we now inhabit. At some point in the history of our incarnations we were everything and, therefore, experienced everything. Consequently, there is a very great chance that we made vows, we were cursed, and also that we cursed others.

In the kibbutz society where I was raised, there was no space for vows and curses. Beyond the fact that no one talked about these things, no one believed in them, either. In fact, it wasn't until I was 26, when I was studying energy healing, that I learned how to work with the "evil eye" for the first time. Until then, all these "evil eye"-type things, vows and curses, seemed primitive and did not belong to my world. Entering the energy world taught me otherwise. However, in over 15 years of energy work, I did not deal with curses and vows. They just didn't show up in my clinic and, in truth, there's a chance that even if they had presented in plain sight, I wouldn't have necessarily recognized them.

On one occasion, as part of The Systemic Lab, which I detailed in the introduction, I began to practice constellation work with the Akashic records. During the investigation in the lab with a group of women who came to explore with me, as I was examining how and if it was possible to work with the Akashic records, one of the participants asked to examine the subject of her romantic relationships.

Iris was a widow in her late fifties. She was widowed at a young age and since then had been unable to find a new relationship. Everything ended as soon as it began. No relationship seemed able to last. We met in The Systemic Lab. This was one of the first meetings where we investigated working with the Akashic records. Iris's topic was romantic relationship. We placed a representative for Iris, for the Akashic records, and for Relationship. A story emerged.

In a previous incarnation, Iris was the priest of some god. The representatives in the constellation stood in for all the representations, but nothing moved. The session was stuck. When nothing moves in a constellation, it is a sign that there is a vow. We brought a representation for the vow, and then the full story came out. Iris, in a previous life, made a vow of abstinence. She vowed to devote herself to worshipping God and not to let members of the opposite sex distract her.

This vow had accompanied her ever since, and is reflected in this incarnation in the fact that she had not been able to form a long-lasting intimate relationship since she was widowed. When we freed her from the vow and separated the incarnations, Iris breathed a sigh of relief. In the six months following the session, Iris found a relationship that was right for her and still, years later, lasting.

From Iris's session I learned that vows are above karma. They are like a force that trumps everything. No matter what you planned as a soul in this incarnation, if there is a vow, it will direct your plans. So, if in a previous life, you made a monastic vow of some kind and, in this lifetime, you choose to be a parent—you may not be able to conceive. There could be difficulty finding a partner, or something will go wrong with parenting. Why? Although you've made agreements with other souls, a vow is like a buffer between you and all your plans. It's like a tattoo on the soul—a tattoo that dictates your conduct, a tattoo that needs to be removed.

Over time, I've learned that vows are not so rare and that often, when people experience a great stagnation in their lives, it is the product of a vow of some kind.

What Is a Vow?

In the process of working on the book, I received a beautiful message from The Group that explains, in the deepest and most eloquent way, what a vow is, how it works, and what its implications are for our lives in and beyond the current incarnation. I chose to present to you the channeled message in its entirety here:

The world is full of vows and promises. Sometimes the gap between vows and promises is very small and sometimes enormous. Politicians, for example, keep making promises to you, you believe them and they don't fulfill those promises, and that's okay with you. So what happens when someone promises something, and it stays in the system? Why is a vow not like a promise? And how is it affected by who it's made to? Does every vow that a clergyman makes to God count? What makes one vow count and another vow not count?

First of all, how deep is the vow? How directly does it stem from the world of emotions? Because you, dear souls, are not really souls; when you are on this Earth you are human. How deep is your intention, your devotion, to change, avenge, create a new way of life? The deeper the intention, and the more the promise is made with that intention, the more binding the vow.

Politicians don't pay for the vows they made to their constituents and broke, not in this incarnation and not in the next; they pay differently, if at all. But vows, a bit like curses, forged from deep feelings of anger, frustration, helplessness, desperation, or love, stay with you. This is because you have taken on a deep commitment, and that commitment serves you in the incarnation in which you made the vow. Afterwards, this commitment becomes like a chain on your feet; it burns into your consciousness and affects your soul.

We do not say not to make vows. A person needs vows; they give them confidence. One of the reasons you make vows, dear people, is because these vows give you certainty.

Take, for example, the mother who vows to God that if He heals her child she will repent, stop doing certain things, and start doing all kinds of other things. This promise endows her with the confidence that her child will heal.

Or take the woman who vows not to have children in order to punish her husband, because she has no other way out of her unhappy marriage and does not want to have children in this marriage and also does not want her husband to enjoy the fruits of his bad conduct. Even if he hurts her, even if he forcibly takes her to his bed, this woman, when she vows, projects a deep intention to defend herself, to protect those who are not yet created, and to harm, yes, also to harm that man. This focused intention gives her certainty, it comforts her during difficult nights, it allows her to continue to conduct herself within the confines of the terror in which she lives. This is what makes the promise a vow that follows her later to other incarnations.

We are not here to tell you not to make vows, or put your hands on the Bible, the New Testament, the Koran, or any holy object on which you want to vow. These vows, when you supposedly swear on your holy book, are vows that do not pass with you; they are matters that do not interest the world of souls. But when a vow is conceived with an intention, and that intention emanates from the depths of despair or frustration or love, the vow is fixed. When these are love vows, most of the time the vows you give to your loved ones stem from an intention that rests upon fear, loss, and the desire to create certainty.

When a woman tells her partner on his deathbed, "I vow that I will never marry" or "I will look for you in other lives," what she does, in fact, is create certainty, and she sets the course of her life. At that moment, she receives the certainty that she lacks because the pain of the passing of a loved one is unbearable, but she looks at the present moment and the pain she is experiencing with great love. We take our hats off to her for this love, for this transcendence. Not all human beings manage to reach this level of love and enlightenment, from the place of fear of what will happen, of a future without the beloved. But this woman has. And from this place of strength she creates her own reality. That is why vows walk you across periods, whole lifetimes, and constitute this life.

We will now say something Yael did not know: a vow reincarnates in the same gender in which it originated and in similar life situations. If a woman makes a vow, it will reemerge when the soul reincarnates again as a woman. The energetic experiences in the male gender are different from the energetic experiences in the female gender and, therefore, vows will often appear according to the gender you are, or according to the experiences you have had in that gender and the vows you have made as that gender.

— The Group

Cumulative Vows

The idea of "cumulative vows" is new information that came to me through The Group. It arrived, among other reasons, to explain how priestly or monastic vows, which are often formed out of life circumstances rather than from true and fervent faith, affect future lives. I find this explanation to be significant as I have seen how monastic vows have affected souls in this life and have wondered how they work, when not everyone who makes vows actually does so out of genuine passion and commitment.

I know that for many lifetimes I was a nun and here, in this life, I am married with three children. That is, my previous monastic vows haven't affected me (at least not in this incarnation). The question of when and whom they do affect has engrossed me ever since I discovered the power of vows over karma.

~~~~~~

There is a thing called a "cumulative vow," which also affects your life. A cumulative vow is a priestly vow, an oath to a certain way of life, which sometimes has a genuine intention and commitment to doing actions in the presence of the divine. But sometimes there are those who follow this path because it is customary, because this is where they were sent, or because food and shelter is provided in temples, churches, and monasteries.

Vows of abstinence, priestly vows, do not always contain the same intentions as in the previous vows we gave as example, but if you have taken these vows incarnation after incarnation they become part of the basis of your memories. You remember that this is what you did. That's why they affect you, that's why they're there. If you made a vow of abstinence, to living a life of modesty or purity, reincarnation after reincarnation, and you may have been a priest or you may have been a Buddhist or you may have been both, and the religion you practiced may no longer exist today, but if you have moved from the worship of one god to another, from one asceticism to another, this is more of a pattern than a vow that goes with you. It manages you on a subconscious level.

In this case, we would suggest, also to Yael, to look at the incarnations in which this pattern was created, in which these vows were created, to pay attention to the story that led to the reason why in every incarnation the same person went to a monastery, to a mosque, to any other worship of God, and why that man or woman became a monk or a nun. What was there for them—in every incarnation, not just in one? To see the incarnations, to understand the story that led people to make such vows, and from this place, the influence of these incarnations, the power of these vows, will gradually decrease, for if we understand the motivation behind the soul of the person, it ceases to control them.

You are a person blessed with emotions and intentions that have sometimes led you astray. We invite you to air your feelings and motivations and intentions and generate new energy from them. Take what you've gone through and learn from it, rather than seeing it as something that's holding you back in life. And whatever you do, we wish you nothing but the best for your path. Nothing that has been signed in the past has to affect you now. That is our blessing for you.

Best wishes, The Group

How Do You Change Vows?

The intensity of the energy contained in a vow is what allows it to traverse incarnations. Marriage vows, for example, are exciting, but they do not contain pain, passion, hatred, or any other energy experienced with great intensity; therefore, they do not pass with us to other incarnations.

Vows of revenge, on the other hand, remain—along with vows of loss, fear, or pain, or those made by nuns. They follow us across incarnations and last from the moment they were created to the present day, affecting our lives, our soul contracts, and our karma. When the source of the vow is discovered, it can be freed from our current incarnation. When this happens, its grip on our karma disappears, and we can go on with our lives, without the blockage that the vow had created.

The soul cannot free itself from the vows we have made. Since vows are made in the body, they are allowed through when we manifest in the body. As a soul, I cannot break free from a vow made during any incarnation, but as a human being, I can break this vow.

Following the message I received on the subject of taking vows, The Group conveyed the following message:

We leave it in the hands of Yael's constellation or any therapist who knows how to make room for the pain of that incarnation. That's all. All you have to do is acknowledge the pain and fear of that woman on her deathbed, the pain and fear of the woman whose husband is abusing her, the pain and fear of the woman whose child is lying in the hospital. These are, for the most part, the vows that stay in your life.

— The Group

I believe that each of us has the power to break free from the vows we have made ourselves and no one needs a cleric to release them.

Yashika's Story

"I'm 44 years old and unmarried. None of my relationships have been serious. I want that to change."

"Do you want to be married?" I ask her.

"Yes," she replies.

We begin to place representations—of her, the soul, and the relationship.

Everything feels heavy and stuck.

To her.

And to me, too.

The representations stay still, and I have no idea which representations are relevant.

Is it a soul lesson?

Is it a soul contract?

Nothing feels clear, and it is also hazy to me who or what the lesson or contract is, so I keep asking her to stand in for the representations. When she stands in for her soul, she feels that there is a barrier—something is blocked. I decide to check what that is. She brings a representation of the barrier. Now everything becomes clear—there is a vow involved. There is a vow in the system and a vow, as I have just learned, trumps everything. We add a representation of the vow, and the system starts shifting.

I ask her to represent those who made the vow in that lifetime. She stands in for the representation, and I ask her what the representation suggests to her. The information that emerges from the representation is a promise/vow not to have children.

"To whom do you make this promise?" I ask her. "A husband, father, anyone else?"

"Husband," she replied.

I ask her to bring a representation of the husband in the previous life. I'm trying to figure out what kind of karmic story is going on here. Did she deprive her husband of children and now lives a life in which she is deprived (at least to this day) of children?

Maybe.

It's not clear enough to me, so I switch tacks and focus on releasing the present from the hold of the vow. This does the trick. The previous incarnation takes responsibility—the person who made the vow takes ownership for it and releases the soul in its current incarnation and even blesses her with a relationship and children. A movement of rapprochement is created. All the feelings of heaviness and immobility with which the constellation began have dissipated, and there is a connection between the soul and the current incarnation and relationship.

The karmic law is not always clear to me or revealed during the constellation. I don't always know if it's a lesson of the soul, a soul contract, or something else, but it's not that significant to me. I am primarily interested in one, sole principle—disentangling—that is, freeing—the present life from the past version of us who made the vow.

A vow establishes karma, prevents lessons and learning, and constrains the soul's progress. When a vow is released or removed, the soul can realize its potential. It is no longer bound by the shackles of past intention and expired energy from the incarnation in which the vow was made.

After vows appeared and I learned to work with them, curses began to enter my world.

Curses

Since the dawn of time there has been evidence of curses. Curses are meant to protect and deter. For example, whoever enters Pharaoh's tomb will have their life ruined. This curse is meant to protect the tomb and its treasures. I believe that as the work of priesthood and healing improved and people saw that priestly and medical men had powers, these men were used to produce curses whose purpose was not only protection and resentment but revenge. Of course it wasn't just priests and witches who engaged in healing arts. The Karmic Constellation showed me that a curse doesn't require a professional; it is often made up of other things.

Energy has different frequencies. A curse is a way to take energy and impose a certain frequency upon it. Humans initially thought that nature was cursing them; that they were punished. This led to the understanding that there is such a thing as curses. The more humankind learned to master the world of elements—Fire, Water, Earth, and Air—the more magic and curses were created. (Although this book is not about witchcraft, and I view spells as different from curses, the work of the curse and that of the sorcerer is often the same.)

The work of the curse is a concoction of elements, sometimes physical or material and sometimes purely energetic. What unites it and turns a curse into a curse is the intention and the intensity of the energy it contains. Curses that affect incarnations are curses that hold within them a true, pure, painful, or fearful intention. The greater the intensity of the pain and the greater the intention, the more weight the curse holds.

This is what The Group said about curses:

Cursing is a very human invention. Emotionally it's a very interesting thing, a very unique experience for humankind. Curses are an accumulation of a lot of energy. It's not just anger, it's not just hatred, it's like a whole Gestalt. It's this place where one emotion is so strong that another emotion begins, a genuine, sincere and unaware desire for its abilities, its strengths, a real desire to hurt. We tend to attribute curses to witches or some mystical abilities, but one doesn't have to be a witch to curse and, even in ancient times, witches didn't necessarily practice curses, nor did wizards. Curses are also not necessarily related to black magic. Curses are associated with a very deep essence of wanting to hurt another. And it is this desire that extends; it is this force that lands on the other person. People curse all the time in this world of yours; in every environment there is a curse. Every child says "I wish you dead" to their mother or father or teacher, and it still does not happen and does not stick, because there is no real desire there; in fact, there is only mild frustration or anger.

A true curse, one that manifests and travels through time, is one that combines more than one emotion of anger, because it contains a bubbling bowl and is, therefore, often attributed to witches. It really does have a bubbling bowl of sensations and emotions, which are all what you call "low frequency" or "negative frequency," and yet, it also has a genuine desire to hurt.

A curse is the loud and powerful cry of a person who has been hurt, a person who feels helpless, who feels that their injury is not being seen.

Often in soul work the soul does not understand its responsibility for this issue, so it goes with it. Only when the soul, the essence as expressed in this incarnation or in the previous incarnation in which it was cursed, can see what was created within it, what it actually created, is there no need for the curse energy.

To what is this similar? To a child who shouts, "Look at me, look at me, look at me," and when his parents don't see him, his cries intensify. If it began with only crying or shouting, "You're not okay," it can end with doors slamming and with parents feeling increasingly wrong. Instead of looking at the child and asking, "How can I see you? How can I help you?" and witnessing the child, going through a process that helps to witness the child, because only then healing can occur, most people stay rooted in their own point of view, "He's wrong, I gave the child everything." You didn't see them fully and acknowledge everything they have asked you to. This analogy is the essence of a curse, an indication that someone has been hurt. When you see this, the curse will be released from your energy. It travels with you; it is merely a sign of a time of blindness, a sign of a great pain that you created.

Curses, as we said at the beginning, are a very interesting invention of the human race. They are mirrors, most poignantly showing the power of pain that a person experiences. They highlight how much power pain has, that out of pain the life of another can be ruined.

— The Group

For a curse to work, it needs to meet the energy of the cursed. A person cannot be cursed if there is no place exposed to the curse, if they don't have faith that they should be cursed, if they don't feel guilty. A small hole in our aura or astral field, something small inside us that is open to a curse, is enough for it to attack in full force. This is an unconscious process.

A person who believes in curses, witchcraft, and that evil or low energies can affect them can go through life with a curse. A person who has committed an offensive act and has, on a certain level (can be on a soul level), guilty feelings or remorse can be influenced by curses.

Shelly's Story

"I want to work on my relationships in general, not a particular relationship or anything specific," she tells me.

We lay out fabric representations of her, the soul, and relationship, and we begin the session.

From the beginning of the session, the way the fabrics (or representations) are placed, one can see that she and the soul are on one carpet and the relationship is on another (Shelly's space is filled with carpets, and the representations are placed on the carpets rather than directly on the floor).

Two things catch my attention:

1 There is no connection between the elements, between Shelly's representative and "my soul," and vice versa. Nor is there any connection between the two of them and the representation of relationship.
2 When we add the soul lesson to the field, the relationship wants to be disruptive and harmful.

This surprises me because we placed a representation for the soul lesson related to relationship and I didn't expect malice to come out of the representation of relationship. Yes, it seems logical to me that emotions such as pain, sadness, distance, detachment, would appear, but not evil, nor the desire to inflict harm. Beyond that, the soul and the lesson felt paralyzed and unable to move.

What could it be?, I wondered to myself.

Usually when there is a powerful stagnant energy in the system it is either a vow or a curse, but why would anyone vow not to have relationships at all? That doesn't make sense to me. And why would the representation of the relationship want to interfere and cause harm? That doesn't make sense, either.

So we test my hypothesis that there is a curse involved. I ask Shelly to place a representation of the curse. We discover that, in another life, someone cursed Shelly to not feel like she belonged, and it has been that way ever since. That's not what she came to learn in this incarnation, but the curse dictated her conduct. When we do a process with that incarnation, the curse is lifted and a connection is created between "the soul" and "mine," as well as a connection to relationship that has not been there before; then, relationship feels light and fun, and opens up to Shelly, and she too feels open to it.

The curse, along with the cursers, remains on another carpet and Shelly, the soul, the lesson, and relationship find themselves together on the same carpet, a small, intimate, and connected group, which is exactly what Shelly has been wishing for herself.

Curses from the Perspective of Karmic Constellation

In the beginning of my career I didn't pay any attention to curses at all. In general, in my life as Yael, I give them less credence and believe that they are more typical of certain populations, certain places, and certain periods, and I do not take part in any of them.

But the Karmic Constellation has no limits.

In addition, a curse is an expression of a desire to do evil— when a person curses someone, they do not curse them to abundance, they curse them to illness, poverty, loneliness, loss, and so on. So, with Shelly, when "relationship wanted to hurt my soul," it occurred to me that it was a curse. I discovered in the Karmic Constellations that although a person, the soul, has karma, a curse, like a vow, stands above karma. It affects karma and affects a person's life, even if it was uttered many incarnations ago.

One of the questions I am often asked is why curses are reincarnated with us and how they are released. Here's what The Group had to say on this subject:

A genuine desire to hurt often stems from the fact that
the person has been hurt, not because they have powers
and are vicious and cruel in their original essence.
The very ability to see that the perpetrator is actually
the victim already diminishes the frequency of the curse,
diminishes the perspective of the bystander, even the
point of view of the one who is cursed, since the one who
is cursed did an act, whether knowingly or in good faith or
blindly, an act that harmed the person who cursed them.
— The Group

When this happens, the energy of the curse dissolves, disappears, and ceases to be a burden that the soul takes on. I believe that curses go through reincarnations with us, because the soul does feel guilty for what happened and takes the curse upon itself. In fact, it is an experience of guilt that creates a feeling that something is not coming. And so the soul and the person are reduced and do not live life to the fullest.

I have discovered in my work that, in dealing with curses, both the cursed and the curser are locked in the energy of the curse. Unlike a vow, which is an energy that only the person who makes a vow "carries," in the case of curses, both the cursed and the curser "carry" the energy with them over time and through incarnations.

What can one do? How does one let it go?

By taking responsibility. Taking responsibility is a refining move. When the soul takes responsibility for what happened, when the previous incarnation, or we in the present incarnation, understand what the hurt was and acknowledge it along with the pain we created, the energy of the curse dissolves. Since everything that has been cursed usually wants recognition of the pain inflicted on them, the recognition of the pain releases the curse and liberates the shared stagnant energy. I see in Karmic Constellations how true recognition of pain or injury causes the energy of the curse to dissolve and cleanse itself from space, and how this recognition releases energies from those who cursed as well. When these two things happen, the cursed person can be free to live.

———

Next time you're hurting, don't curse. It will hurt you as much as those whom you seek to curse. There are other ways to deal with your pain. There are other ways to deal with or engage with your emotions in a respectful and loving way for your highest good. The question is whether this is the way to appropriately and healthily use the power of one's emotions.

— The Group

Exercise
Dissolving Vows

Many times, we are unaware of vows in our energy field. I have often discovered that the precise moment when a person realizes for certain that there is a vow, this moment actually serves as a soul lesson.

This exercise is designed to work on vows in your energy field. Without needing to know exactly what they affect, it will remove them from your energy and create a big shift inside you and in your behavior.

To start with, bring three representations (you can bring three notes and write a different representation on each note):

- Me in this Lifetime/Incarnation
- My Soul
- A Vow I Made in a Previous Life that Affects Me to This Day

Stand in for each representation twice. You can do so by placing your hand on one of the notes and, each time, place one hand on a different representation. Notice the energy present within each representation; become aware of whether it is pleasant or unpleasant, heavy or light, or something else.

If, when you stand in for the representations, you want to move the representations elsewhere, do it.

Once you've moved the representations, notice if anything has changed in your energy.

When you stand in for the vow, pay attention to whether you have an understanding of it. For example, to what topic in your life it is related, the essence of the vow, and so on. If there is no understanding, feeling, or emotion about the representation of the vow, that too is perfectly fine.

Place a representation for the incarnation in which the vow was made, and return to stand in for the other representations.

Notice any changes in the feelings and sensations of any of the representations you have laid out. Especially pay attention if there is a change in the sensations related to the vow.

Add a representation of "Me from the Incarnation in Which the Vow Was Made" and return to the other representations.

Did this addition change any feelings?

Did the different representations you stood in for want to move from their place or change position and has their energy shifted through this?

Have you now become clearer about the vow, its nature, and its effect?

Finally, add the last representation in the exercise: "The Reason Why 'Past Life Me' Made the Vow." And again, go back to the rest of the representations, and notice the difference in sensations, emotions, and locations.

What happens to the energy of the vow now? Is it the same as it was in the beginning of the session, or has it changed? Did it shift or change position?

Beyond the desire to know what the vow is, movement is important. Our soul subconsciously knows which vows we have made and what affects us in the current incarnation. If there is movement in your inner energy, if you feel different at the end of the exercise, or if there is physical movement in the representations, it indicates a change in the energy of the vow, and perhaps even its undoing.

Chapter 8

The Akashic Records and Their Healing Potential

What if there exists a realm that holds all the knowledge a soul has gained throughout its lifetimes? A sacred place where healing, growth, and clarity unfold, guiding the soul's journey. This place is the Akashic Records—timeless, vast, and within reach.

———

The records are a map of your soul. They are a pathfinder, and the more you use them, the clearer and clearer the path will be, and we urge you, implore you, to work through the records, by any means that suits you, in order to open up the knowledge and clear the way. The resources in the records are enormous, even the traumas. Clearing traumas gives way to resources, and as you cleanse more and more, you grow in resource, in your ability to contain this world, so we implore you, dear ones, work with the records, cleanse energies from past lives, clear energies from previous generations, be yourself. The more yourself you are, the more this trait will pass on with you to future generations as well as future incarnations. Now is the time to clear karma.

Working with records is one of the gifts we can offer humanity in order to do this. We look to you with anticipation and excitement to see how you will implement this gift given to you. We are here to support you in whatever move you choose to make.

— The Group

What Are the Akashic Records?

Imagine a huge library or digital cloud where all the things you have ever experienced, learned, done, and thought as a soul are stored; a space or hall where all physical, spiritual, biological, and cognitive knowledge is stored from the day your soul was formed until today. This space is called the Akashic records.

The Akashic records contain sensations, emotions, knowledge, and memories from all the lives we went through as a soul. When the soul descends into the body, it descends with a master plan that details what it wants to experience in this life and what needs to happen in order for it to experience things.

The soul's subconscious contains the Akashic records, and they are intended to support the soul's master plan with lessons and learning it has chosen for this incarnation. Therefore, there will be information that will be accessible to us, and there will be information that will not be accessible. What does accessible information mean? That which comes easily; things we accomplish without much effort and feel comfortable with. Think of Master Chef participants who say they've been in the kitchen from an early age (or even those that entered the kitchen at a relatively older age) and felt at home and, when they began to cook, became flexible thinkers, open and creative.

Accessible information also contains energy that dictates our behavior. It won't necessarily be easy to confront. Difficulties we experience, such as in thought and behavioral patterns, challenges in life, and people we have a hard time with—this information may all be found in the Akashic records. Hypochondria, for example, can be a manifestation of memories from previous lives in which we experienced illness. Although the person in this incarnation is healthy, the Akashic records hold memories of illness, which affect the person and their consciousness.

Inaccessible information, on the other hand, is something that can challenge us. I can make schnitzel for my kids every Saturday and still need to refer to the recipe, and each time feels like the first time. I have no connection or love for the kitchen, and I do things in the kitchen because I have to, not because I love to. The knowledge of previous times when I loved being in the kitchen— if there were any such times—is inaccessible to me.

In the hypochondriac example, all the incarnations of that soul in which it was healthy are blocked. The mass of the energy of sickness is greater or more significant than the mass of energy of health and, therefore, deep knowledge of health is inaccessible to that person.

Inaccessible information can contain qualities and attributes that we want to introduce into our lives but don't know how to.

Ronit's Story

Ronit arrived at my practice with a strong sense of not belonging, of loneliness. This was her life experience in this incarnation. Ronit saw her past lives and realized that in all her previous lives she had been lonely and didn't belong. This was the information that was available to her, and she experienced her life based on this information. We brought a representation for the Akashic records. When she represented the records, I asked her if there was an incarnation where she felt she belonged, where she wasn't alone.

New knowledge arrived. "Yes!"

A complete incarnation appeared before her. In that incarnation she had a family and was a beloved child. The experience of "belonging" and being "beloved" had not been accessible to Ronit until the moment she represented the records, and together we unblocked the connection to this old/new knowledge.

Where Are the Akashic Records?

~~~

You are born and seemingly start all over again; you have to learn to eat, to talk, to discover how this world works, to learn, to feel, to think, to read. It's an illusion, beloved, an illusion in its entirety. You don't need to attain what you already are, but you don't know that you already are complete. Throughout your incarnations, you have collected and accumulated experiences. They are all within you. You have some perception that the records are outside of you, that you need to meditate and enter, to go outside of yourself into some other space where knowledge is, where the Book of Life is, and maybe many other books. But no, beloveds. What if we tell you that the records are within you? You are the Book of Life.

Unlike a toddler who slowly learns to eat, to play with others, who has a way of developing, who has a natural trajectory of development, you already know. Look at the animals. We've said it more than once and to more than one medium: The animal kingdom's knowledge is great. They do not need to learn, nature lies within them, the knowledge that they must wander, how to wander and where to wander is within them, even though no one has ever led them on this journey. The Akashic records are within you, in every single cell within you. You are the Book of Life, and you don't have to make an effort to get there. That's why it's so easy to stand in for a representation, a piece of fabric or a note, and become the entity it represents. You are your own records.

Yes, there is a reason why not all is open to you from birth. The knowledge is great. It can overwhelm, and the human body—the newborn baby and the nervous system, which is a physiological biological entity—cannot contain this amount of information. That's why the information is hidden from you. But as you get older, as you grow and your nervous system can contain more information, you can easily access the records. It is possible through a teacher, it is possible on your own, it is possible through a Karmic Constellation, and it is possible through other means. The records are yours, and they are accessible to each and every one of you. All you need to do is ask to open up to the knowledge that is you. The records, as Yael wrote, are neutral. They hold all the knowledge and are, therefore, the greatest potential tool for healing that you have. You are who you are by virtue of everything you have been through, everything you have gone through in this and other lives, as well as your intergenerational memory. Through the ages, everything is recorded in the records. So accessing the records, understanding what is in them that can strengthen you or can hold you back, and working with that knowledge can bring great healing.

— The Group

Changing Karma and the Akashic Records

The Akashic records are not about changing karma. Working with them is not about changing karma directly. That being said, access to the information contained within the records allows for healing and change of perspective and, when this happens, it is possible to change karma as well.

When I started to write this book, I debated whether or not to include a chapter about the records. The reason I decided to include them in the book is that, to me, the records are very meaningful. Working with them has changed my life. In working with the records, I developed the Karmic Constellation method and, thanks to my spiritual guidance (which is found in the records) this book was written. I see working with the Akashic records and karmic work as intertwined. I regard my encounter with the records as an encounter with the deepest layers of myself.

One of the things that prevents us from changing our lives is the traumas found in the records that unconsciously dictate our lives, as well as the fact that healing and empowering information is not readily accessible to us. When I work with the records, both through the Karmic Constellation and other tools,

I open up to the information that exists there, create accessibility, and cleanse traumas from past lives.

When traumas from past lives are resolved, the energy in the records changes. The mass of what affects us also changes and we open up, both energetically and in our tangible lives, to new thoughts, feelings, and patterns of behavior.

The knowledge in the records drives your actions, who you are, your essence, your likes and dislikes, your loves, your hate, all the obstacles you encounter and also all of your successes. You draw everything from the records.

What is changing karma? Changing karma is getting out of the place you're in and moving elsewhere. It is to stop suffering, for example. It is to love differently. It is to be yourself in a way you didn't know you could be. It's connecting to deeper, gentler, more loving layers within you.

Some of the knowledge is in the records. Some of the knowledge of karma change will be new to you.

The records, when cleansed of the energy of traumas, can support you in your progress. Your attitude towards and relationship with the records is yours to cultivate. Your attitude towards the knowledge in the records is yours. Will you choose to connect with it and learn from it? Will you choose to connect with it and clear the energies that manipulate and control you, which you don't even know are affecting you? Will you seek to connect and gain new knowledge? Will you choose to connect to dimensions that you do not experience in your life today but have experienced in the past?

The records are there. They are open to you. All they require is an approach and a route to access them. They are in service of humans and their personal development. They don't change karma. What you do with the information you receive from them is what can change your karma.

We hope that more clarity has been created about the role of the records in changing your life as a human being and the power you have to bring about change in your life. The power is within you, in your decisions, in their implementation, in choosing to go in and learn more about yourself from yourself. We are here to support you.

— The Group

How to Work with the Akashic Records

In my book, *Bringing Healing into Your Life: Tools for Working with the Akashic Records*, I detail in-depth tools and ways with which you can work with the records. In this chapter, I will present the main techniques.

There are several ways to work with the records: you can attain knowledge and guidance from them, bring healing to the traumas that are stored in the records, and connect to the resources that are in the records and call them into your life.

Since the records are like a huge library, it is possible to extract from them information on various topics that concern us. We can see/experience different incarnations and gain greater insights into our lives and soul journey. We can connect to our spiritual guides, who are in the record, and work with them to get new information and guidance for our lives in the present.

One can go about connecting to knowledge and guidance by various modes: meditation, attunement, channeling. Each person has tools they know and that are comfortable for them.

Healing for Traumas Found in the Records

Working with the Akashic records allows us access to specific events that created trauma that is controlling us in the present moment. Engaging with these events, understanding what happened, and releasing the traumatic energy from that incarnation and soul memory enables healing on deep levels and changes life in the present.

Neta's Story

Neta does not attend constellation sessions, but has been coming to me for psychotherapy sessions for the past six months. We are working on various issues related to, among other things, her father. Neta arrives at the clinic and tells me a story about her father and money.

I hear the story and check in with myself about how this relates to the soul lesson and past lives. But we hadn't scheduled a constellation session, and our time together is shorter than a regular constellation session. How can it be done in a short time, I wonder?

"Let's work directly with the Akashic records," I suggest to her.

There's something about working with the Akashic records on a particular topic that evokes all energies from all incarnations (past and present) in one session and that can often take less time than a full constellation session.

We place a representation in the space: for her, for her soul, for her father's soul, and for the Akashic records. From the records, sensations emerge: potential, heaviness, and fatigue.

I ask her to bring representations for each of these feelings. She stands in for each representation and examines which feelings arise. At one point, she puts her father's soul behind one of the representations and stands in for it. I decide to stand in for the representation of the father's soul, mainly to give her the feeling that there is someone behind the representation she currently stands in for. But I can't stand in for the representation without immediately connecting to it and starting to represent it myself.

I get the feeling of a very strong connection, as if we are bound by a certain energy. As a facilitator, I know that feeling—it's the feeling of a vow.

I step off the representation and ask Neta to return to the Akashic records. When she stands in for and is representing the records, I ask her, "Is there a vow in the relationship between you and your father?" She says yes.

We bring a representation for the vow.

I ask her to stand in for the representation of fatigue and pay attention to what is happening there. Slowly, a story comes up—a story about another incarnation where she was the daughter and her father was her father.

We bring representations of her in the previous life and her father in the previous life. The story that arises there is very similar to the story in the present. There is a weak, lifeless father and a daughter full of life.

Family constellations teach us that when a child has a feeling that they are in some way more than their parents, it is frightening and many times, as children, we will give up our sense of power and life in order not to be more than our parents and/or to heal our parents. It something like: "I'll give you my power and then you'll have the power to be my parent."

She stands in for the representation of her in that incarnation and understands the vow she made. She talks about the vow and then looks at herself in her incarnation today and takes responsibility for the vow.

As I mentioned, vows have a tendency to reincarnate over space and time.

The representation of potential teaches us that one of the reasons they reincarnated together in this incarnation was to bring healing and change to what was created in that previous incarnation, in order to cancel the vow, and also so that this time the girl does not give up her power for her father. It's a process. The first step is to release the vow from that incarnation. The second step is to release the vow from this incarnation and then agree to be more than our parents.

To see if there really has been a change, I ask her to stand in for the representation of fatigue. She stands there, and there is a sense of silence and neutrality. There are no longer unpleasant sensations like there were before. When that happens, I know a change has occurred.

Unpleasant feelings let us know that there is a story there. When the story is revealed, and the energy stored within it is released and acknowledged, the unpleasant feelings undergo transformation.

Just before our time ends, we perform a small ritual. We burn the incense of sage and release energy from past and current lives.

Something else was released in her connection with her dad: another step on the way to emotional independence that will lead to independence in other aspects of her life.

Connecting to Resources from
Past Lives or Forgotten Memories

A resource is anything that gives us power. In the language of working with trauma, a resource can be a memory of something good we experienced; for example, a positive experience we had or a hobby. When we connect to resources, our resilience grows and so does our ability to cope with life.

In addition, connecting to resources can serve as a path to changing behaviors. Because the records contain all the knowledge, they also contain all the times we did succeed in our tasks—times we overcame difficulties, times we coped. When we are exposed to this knowledge, on a cognitive, emotional, and experiential level, it balances the knowledge of all the times we did not succeed or were traumatized. Instead of sticking with our tendency to look at "what isn't" we get a heaping dose of "what is" and that, in and of itself, often changes our life path.

Additionally, resources allow us to open up and permit ourselves to be exposed to new qualities and abilities that we would like to introduce into our lives—qualities that may be new to us in this incarnation, but there is a chance that in previous lives were at our disposal and now all we need is to open up within ourselves to the possibility of connecting with them. Connecting to the records to open up to resources facilitates that possibility.

In January 2018, I did my first constellation session with the Akashic records. I did it to myself. I wanted to see if it was even possible to work with the records through representation work. My theme was belonging. The goal was to bring healing to the feeling of isolation that had accompanied me my whole life. I stood in for the Akashic records and, from them, I extracted ten life stories related to belonging. Each story was given a piece of felt to represent it. I didn't know what the stories were and just put the pieces of felt on the floor.

I was as curious as I was skeptical. I stood on the first piece of felt and saw a picture from my childhood: the kibbutz. A memory came to me of a poem I wrote that was posted in the kibbutz's dining room. I remembered the excitement that gripped me when it happened. I felt like I belonged. I felt part of the whole, and I felt seen. These are all feelings that I didn't have often on the kibbutz.

This memory disappeared from my conscious experience because it didn't fit the narrative I told myself about the kibbutz—that I didn't belong. But here, the records showed me a moment in my life when I did feel like I belonged. My heart pounded with excitement. I was surprised. I wasn't expecting this.

The rest of the pieces of felt evoked different feelings and sensations, and some also told stories from previous lives. I admit that I don't remember what else the pieces of felt came up with. The first memory, as a child on the kibbutz, surprised and moved me so much that it was etched in my heart and consciousness and overshadowed the others.

Working with the Akashic records as a resource can be done to reinforce qualities that exist within us. Here is an example of the process of entering records, which I put in place to strengthen qualities of giving and receiving.

During COVID-19, I led healing meditations once a week. From time to time we worked with the records. The theme of one particular meeting was giving and receiving: I entered the Akashic records to strengthen within myself the ability to give and receive without guilt or apology.

First image
I see a moneylender. He weighs gold coins on scales. He tells me: "This is my livelihood. It's legitimate. I'm allowed to earn and make a living." I experience the unapologetic masculine energy, and it moves me. This man is me in another life. I bring this energy into my awareness, into my being.

Second image
A boy steals an apple from the market and hides to eat it. I wonder how giving and receiving relate to theft. He tells me, "If I don't eat, I'll die." In fact, he cares about his life. He is taking in order to survive.

I ask him about the future. Whether in the future, when he is grown up, he would have any qualms about the theft. He looks at me and says, "I don't know if I'll make it to becoming a grown-up."

I understand. Life is here and now. The instinct for life is greater than anything else, and taking in order to live is not wrong.

Third image
I see nature: cows in meadows—lots of meadows—trees, lots of green. I have no body, I'm just energy, and nature shows me balance. The tree does not apologize to the sun for taking in its light. The cows make no apologies for eating the grass. In nature, the balance is perfect. Nature takes, receives, and gives according to its needs. No more and no less. Only man violates this balance.

I leave the records, integrate all the knowledge I have received in the physical body, and finish the meditation. I feel that something in me has changed—something in the way I look at giving and receiving and my desire to give; the way I give has changed.

In this meditation session I went into the records and met myself in a previous life. Each such encounter taught me something about myself and something about receiving and taking without guilt. My knowledge from previous lives combined with the knowledge from this incarnation and together became greater. In addition, the experience of receiving and taking without guilt grew within me, as did my sense of worthiness.

Exercise
Resources

Think about an issue with which you have some difficulty. It can be money, self-image, relationships, parenting, or anything else.

Bring representations for:

- Me in This Incarnation
- My Soul
- The Subject

Stand or place your hand on each representation for 30 seconds to a minute, and pay attention to the sensations, feelings, and even thoughts and images that arise.

Bring a representation for the Akashic records.

Ask the Akashic records how many incarnations you have had in which you have experienced the exact opposite of the current incarnation. For example, if you don't earn enough money, ask for incarnations where you lived in financial comfort and earned enough money. If you have low self-esteem, ask for reincarnations where you believed in yourself and were confident, and so on.

The records will give you a number. It can be one incarnation or several hundred. My recommendation: If it's up to 10 incarnations, bring in as many representations as incarnations. If the number is over 10 incarnations, bring one representation for every 10 incarnations.

Place the representations of the incarnations. Before you stand in for them, go back to standing in for the representation of "me," then of the soul, and then of the subject, and notice if anything has changed following the entrance of the incarnation.

Sometimes that in itself is enough.

Now stand in for each incarnation and ask yourself: What do I feel/sense? What was it about this incarnation that allowed me to flourish (to make money, to be confident, and so forth)? How does it feel? Speak aloud or write down what it was and how it felt.

Imagine that the representation of a previous life is giving you this experience as a gift and that you are open to receiving it. Every single cell in your body opens up to this knowledge and memory of who you were in a previous life.

Remember that whoever you were in a previous life has gained knowledge that you are entitled to. By virtue of being the same soul, the knowledge of the previous incarnation is also yours.

Follow this process for every incarnation. You will find that each incarnation has its own story, feelings, and sensations and a completely different frequency.

Go back to the original issue. How is it feeling now? Does it have the same sensations as it did in the beginning?

And when you stand in for your soul, what has changed?

And how about "me"? What is the feeling there now?

Working with the Akashic records is working directly with the incarnations and everything that has caused us to act as we do today. We open ourselves to knowledge that existed but was hidden—knowledge that controlled us or knew that, if given to us, we could manage our lives more easily.

The records are part of us, and they control us on a daily basis through our subconscious. The more we gain knowledge about what they are and the more we bring healing to the records themselves or through the records, the more we reduce their unconscious influence and strengthen our connection to the resources that exist within them.

CONCLUSION

When I was instructed by my guidance to write a book, I resisted. The two previous books I published had required the investment of much time and energy, and I didn't have the strength to begin this journey once more. The guidance allayed my fears and told me that all my material already existed. All I needed to do was gather it; I wouldn't need to write new things.

Never believe your guidance. It seduces you with small objectives so that great things will emerge from you.

This book has been a journey.

It was a journey of growth and clarity, of sharpening the knowledge that exists within me, and of receiving new knowledge. It allowed me to deepen the teachings in Karmic Constellation courses and make them accessible, not only to my students but to the whole world. It also helped me reconnect with other forms of channeling and gain a broader, sometimes wholly new, knowledge base of the world of souls and, through them, of this world, too.

Writing the book has opened me up to a deeper connection with myself and a deeper trust of my guidance.

It is my hope that in reading this book, you too feel connected to yourselves on deeper levels. I hope you are strengthened by understanding more about who you are and your wondrous essence. I hope you are able to see the soul agreements you've made, examine the lessons you've asked to learn, and perhaps even manage to untie a vow or two.

Our journey is not over. We're always on the way. That being said, the more we imbue ourselves with the frequency of self-love, the more we accept life as it is, and the more we accept it from the perspective of the soul, the easier it will be for us to conduct ourselves in this life.

As with all other chapters, The Group has a few closing words for you, readers:

Dear ones, we thank you for making it this far. For going through your soul's journey with us. We hope that the knowledge given to you by both Yael and us—The Group—has awakened you to more facets of yourself, and supported you in the endeavor to embody and understand who you really are.

We urge you to remember that you are here by choice, and that is why we consider you to be beloved, cherished beings.

Choosing to come to Earth—there's courage in that. There's a mission in that, regardless of your occupation. The very act of being here and the path you are taking is the real mission.

This book is meant to open your eyes and heart to the true consciousness and being that you are. We hope we have helped you to embark upon this mission.

We thank you for listening to your heart and for your willingness to expand your consciousness.

CONCLUSION

We are here to support and accompany you along your way.

You are not alone, and your choices are sacred. All your actions, conscious or otherwise, are appropriate. Know that you are right, in your own way, and lovingly accept your life.

We love you.

— The Group

BIBLIOGRAPHY

These are books and sources of inspiration that appear throughout the book:

Carroll, Lee. *The Journey Home—A Kryon Parable: The Story of Michael Thomas and the Seven Angels*. Carlsbad, CA: Hay House, 1997.

Coelho, Paulo. *Manuscript Found in Accra*. Carlsbad, CA: Hay House, 2013.

Moorjani, Anita. *Dying to Be Me: My Journey from Cancer, to Near Death, to True Healing*. New edition and afterword. Carlsbad, CA: Hay House, 2012/2022.

Newton, Michael. Ph.D. *Journey of Souls: Case Studies of Life between Lives*. Llewellyn Publications. Woodbury, MN: 1994.

———. *Destiny of Souls: New Case Studies of Life between Lives*. Woodbury, MN: 2017.

Talbot, Michael. *The Holographic Universe*. New York: HarperCollins Publisher, Inc: 1991.

And a few more recommendations of resources:

Lee Carroll's official YouTube channel, which channels Kryon: www.youtube.com/@kryonleecarroll3491

Tools to work with the Akashic records: www.yaeleini.com/product-page/bringing-healing-into-your-life-tools-for-working-with-the-akashic-records

My YouTube channel, where you can find Karmic Constellations exercises: www.youtube.com/@yaeleini/videos

ACKNOWLEDGMENTS

First, I want to thank my parents. My journey with them has been tough but, as I get older and uncover more and more soul agreements and soul choices, I understand more and more why I chose them.

So, first of all, thank you to my father, may he rest in peace, for passing on to me his talent and his love of writing. I know that's one of the reasons I chose you as my father.

And to my mother, who never understood me—because our soul's lesson was to learn to live in harmony with disharmony—but she let me be me and stood behind me, in her way, in every decision I made and dream that I conceived.

Ziv, my dear and loving husband who, when I told him that I wanted to work and make a living as an energy healer in a world where everyone thought that energy work was for the few and not a legitimate source of income, gave me the space to do so and became one of my most enthusiastic supporters. I didn't take it for granted then, nor do I today.

To Tamar Genesher, who was my first energy-focused therapy teacher and introduced me to Lee Carroll's books. Tamar is also the translator of Kryon's channeled messages in Israel and, thanks to her, Kryon's words have been accessible to me over the years.

To Lee Carroll, who channels Kryon, and to Kryon, whose words, many times, are the engine for my explorations. Thanks to his words about Akashic records and the ability to change karma, The Systemic Lab began to investigate the issues of Akashic records and changing karma in general and, thanks to this, I "discovered" Karmic Constellations.

To my spiritual guidance which, two years prior to publishing this book, told me that I needed to write my third book. In my wildest dreams, I never imagined that this is what would come to pass. So thank you very much.

To Jenny Schori, my editor, who helped me clarify and elucidate these ideas in a way that would be accessible to others. Through her questions, especially in places where I wasn't able to describe things more clearly, The Group appeared.

To The Group, which made itself known to me at the exact moment when I was open to channeling again and gave me information about the world of souls that even I didn't know.

To Yishai Gaster, my Constellations teacher, who not only taught me Family Constellations and Organizational Constellations and certified me as a Family Constellations teacher but also supported my independent way of exploring and experimenting, bringing me and my content to the world of Constellations.

And finally, to my students and clients—through our work together, the principles of the soul system I knew inside me and rediscovered again and again in the clinic have taken form. In fact, you are the ones who taught me in practice about the soul systems, how they can be changed, and how to exit the cycle of karma.

Thanks to all of you, this book exists.

ABOUT THE AUTHOR

Photo by David Atraktsi

Yael Eini is a therapist, constellation facilitator, teacher, and founder of The Systemic Lab, an innovative platform for practicing Systemic and Karmic constellations.

Yael's training and education include a combined bachelor's degree in psychology and management, with honors, and a master's degree in family counseling, contributing to her highly holistic method. Over the last two decades, she has delved deep into the world of energy, acquiring expertise in techniques like EMF balancing technique, Reiki, Emotional Freedom Technique (EFT), and more. Her qualifications as a group facilitator in the integrative approach and as a Somatic Experiencing Practitioner (SEP), provides her with further tools to integrate into her teachings.

As the developer of the unique Karmic Constellation method, Yael Eini has been teaching this model to students around the world since 2019. She facilitates transformative workshops and speaks at professional conferences worldwide about the life-changing potential of the Karmic Constellation approach.

The author of several books in Hebrew and English, Yael has a commitment to serve as a guiding light in the transformative journey toward personal and collective well-being.

For more information on Yael Eini's work visit:

www.yaeleini.com

Also of Interest from Findhorn Press

Shadow Work for the Soul
Seeing Beauty in the Dark

by Mary Mueller Shutan

Identify and reclaim your shadow and free yourself from collective shadow projections. In this practical and trauma-informed guide to deep shadow work, Mary Mueller Shutan shares shadow work tools and exercises to help you find compassion for your dark side, reconnect with the repressed and abandoned parts of yourself, and reclaim the resiliency and joy of your authentic, whole self.

ISBN 979-8-88850-014-9

Also of Interest from Findhorn Press

Words That Free You
What You Say Is What You Become

by Jacques Martel

The right choice of words can liberate, strengthen, and heal us. Not only are the words and phrases we use an expression of our innermost thoughts, they also influence our well-being and the overall nature of our character. In this easy-to-follow guide, therapist Jacques Martel details how to create a more positive, optimistic, healthy, and happy reality by choosing words filled with freedom, wisdom, and love.

ISBN 978-1-64411-962-4

FINDHORN PRESS

Life-Changing Books

Learn more about us and our books at
www.findhornpress.com

For information on the Findhorn Foundation:
www.findhorn.org

Scan the QR code and save 25% at InnerTraditions.com.
Browse over 2,000 titles on spirituality, the occult, ancient
mysteries, new science, holistic health, and natural medicine.